Strategic marketing

Strategic marketing

A business response to consumerism

ANDREW ROBERTSON

A HALSTED PRESS BOOK

JOHN WILEY & SONS
New York – Toronto

English language edition, except USA and Canada published by
Associated Business Programmes Ltd
17 Buckingham Gate, London SW1

Published in the USA and Canada by
Halsted Press, a Division of
John Wiley & Sons Inc
New York

First published 1978

Library of Congress Cataloging in Publication Data

Robertson, Andrew Beaumont, 1921–
Strategic Marketing

"A Halsted Press book."
Includes bibliographical references.
1. Marketing – Social aspects. 2. Consumer protection. I. Title.
HF5415.R5535 1978 658.8 78–3

ISBN 0–470–26313–X

Typeset by
Computacomp (UK) Ltd
Fort William, Scotland
Printed and bound in Great Britain by
Redwood Burn Limited, Trowbridge & Esher

Contents

Preface

According to orthodox economic theory, the object of production is to maximise consumer satisfaction. The sovereignty of the consumer is ensured by the operation of competitive forces within a market economy. By exercising discriminating choice among a variety of competing suppliers, the consumer optimises his or her living standards.

Real life, as we know, is a little different from the model. Over a growing sector of economic life, the consumer's choice is limited – by the imperfections of competition, or by the steady extension of the monopolistic power of the state and its agents. The rational exercise of consumer choice is too often frustrated by lack of knowledge; ignorance is compounded by the growing technical complexity of products on offer, and is too often deliberately fostered by misleading advertising. Sometimes this ignorance goes so far as to endanger consumers' safety or health.

Thus, of the four basic rights of consumers – safety, choice, information and redress – none can be absolutely guaranteed through the operations of market forces alone. They need buttressing by two other forces: legislation by the state, and an active pro-consumer policy on the part of producers. It is because the latter has too often been lacking in the past that heavy reliance has been placed on the former.

During the post-war period, in most western countries, there has been a growing volume of legislation to protect and promote the interests of consumers. Much of this has been carried against the opposition of manufacturers. Industry feels itself threatened by what it regards as an excessive overload of bureaucratic interference, and the consumerist movement has advanced through a policy of confrontation rather than partnership with producer interests.

All of this is well documented by Andrew Robertson in this book, which provides an excellent guide to the growth of consumerism on both sides of the Atlantic. But the answer to industry's complaints, as he demonstrates very clearly, lies in manufacturers' own hands. The active identification with consumers' interests should be part of firms' own marketing strategy. That is the meaning of the phrase 'Strategic Marketing', which is the title of this book. If the response to consumer demands is positive and innovatory, rather than negative and resentful, not only will the pressure for regulatory legislation and other external measures be diminished; the evidence indicates, as Mr Robertson shows through a number of case studies, that the firm itself will benefit in a strict commercial sense.

In other words, producer and consumer interests can alike be best met through a policy of partnership rather than mutual hostility. That I take to be the underlying message of this excellent book, and it is one which, as chairman of the National Consumer Council, I wholeheartedly endorse. The consumer movement itself has grown up over the last two decades. From a rather narrow middle-class base, it has acquired a social conscience. The National Consumer Council pays special attention in its work to the needs of the poorer, less articulate, disadvantaged consumer. It is important for the health of our society, as well as for the strength of our economy and the buoyancy of industry's balance sheets, that the 'Strategic Marketing' lesson be learned. This is a timely and relevant book, which is to be welcomed by businessmen and consumers alike.

Michael Shanks
National Consumer Council
December 1977

Editor's introduction

Consumer protection: some implications for management

Consumerism and business

The significance of consumerism for business is that the public at large and politicians in particular are no longer prepared to accept that businessmen can be relied upon to serve the consumer without external direction and control. The whole marketing philosophy is being questioned. A recent public enquiry in Britain[1] concluded that 'the idea of consumer sovereignty is fallacious. In truth the producer is dominant and his voice is all powerful. His interests normally prevail over the welfare of the consumer.' At a deeper level consumerism questions the autonomy of businessmen and managers. Peter Drucker has explained its growth in terms of the break-down in communications between producers and their consumers:

> 'Consumerism means that the consumer looks upon the manufacturer as somebody who is interested but who really does not know what the consumer's realities are. He regards the manufacturer as somebody who has not

> made the effort to find out, who does not understand the world in which the consumer lives. The economic and social justification for the existence of businesses returning profit to their stockholders has been their commitment to serving customers. If those customers perceive themselves not as patrons to be served but as resources to be manipulated they will express their resentment both in their purchasing and in their voting behaviour.'[2]

A recent public opinion poll in Britain emphasised the low esteem in which businessmen are held. When the public were asked to select from a list of twelve professions the group which they felt were 'least trustworthy', businessmen came top of the list with twenty-nine per cent; when they were asked to choose those 'most trustworthy', businessmen came last with two per cent!

Consumers as a power group

Consumer protection is usually discussed only in terms of protection against the actions of business. Equally important is the safeguarding of consumer interests against the activities of public bodies and also of organised labour. The scope for consumerism is expanding as these power groups improve their ability to lobby government and to influence the media. Western societies are becoming increasingly organised in terms of interest groups and customers will continue to suffer from the actions of militant unions and insensitive bureaucracies until they learn to act in unison and to have their interests represented with the same force as these other groups.

The level of public dissatisfaction with the actions of businessmen, trade unionists, politicians and public officials has escalated as power has been concentrated in fewer hands, and as organisations have become bigger and their leaders more remote.

Consumerism is one aspect of the individual's reaction

against bigness: big companies which have merged smaller family-owned businesses and have raised prices and sacrificed service to customers in order to improve profits; unions which are willing to interrupt holidays, dislocate transportation, cause shortages of bread and other essential commodities and bring basic industries to a halt in pursuit of higher wages; politicians and public officials who are now separated from their constituents and customers by multi-level organisations in which the individual seeking a service is frequently lost and confused.

Future developments

What does the future hold for consumerism in Europe?

1. *Rapid growth in consumer action*

The demand is already there. European consumers are thoroughly dissatisfied. A study by the European Consumer Associations indicated that one person in two is dissatisfied with what he buys and his treatment as a customer.[3]

One survey by a British newspaper showed that forty per cent of young consumers believe all advertisements are misleading. Another poll by a British publishing organisation suggests that eighty per cent of the British population would like to have more organised consumer protection. And the annual level of complaints about the British Trades Descriptions Act which was expected to be about 50 000 has already reached over 100 000.

Consumer organisations in Western Europe already have a sizeable membership and it is increasing. The major groups are:

Consumers' Association (UK)	600 000
Consumentenbond (Netherlands)	400 000
Stiftung Warentest (West Germany)	200 000
Test Achats (Belgium)	180 000

But one can see their potential for growth in comparison with the US Consumers' Union which has 2 500 000 members and an annual income of $16 million.[4]

2. *More militant and political consumer movements*

So far European consumer organisations have behaved in a moderate way. In the USA and Japan consumer interests have been more prone to exercise their power, e.g. by organising consumer boycotts and by public campaigning.

Leaders are needed with the enterprise and drive to attract funds, expose abuses, develop positive programmes and achieve reforms. Ralph Nader, who pioneered the movement in the USA, now runs a consumerism conglomerate with a budget of $1 million, raised in public donations that average about $15 per person. His activities include: the Center for Study of Responsive Law, which produced the original study group reports; Congress Watch, a group of seven full-time lobbyists with back-up research; the Health Research Group, which has campaigned successfully against food adulteration, and a Tax Reform Group, a think-tank and a lobby for reform of the taxation system.

3. *Product liability legislation*

In American law there has been a shift away from *caveat emptor* whereby the buyer has to prove the unsatisfactory nature of a product or service, towards producer liability, a creed which holds producers 'strictly liable' for any defective products.

The extension of the principle in US Courts can be traced through the increasing numbers of product liability suits. The statistics for recent years were:

1960	50 000
1963	250 000
1970	500 000
1975	1 000 000 (estimated)[5]

It is only a matter of time before these values and concepts are transferred to Western Europe. A draft directive has been issued by the European Commissioners and a discussion paper has been prepared by the English and Scottish Law Commissions. Product liability legislation is now almost a foregone conclusion.

4. *The spread of consumer consultative councils and public interest representation on boards*

Consumer Councils are well established in publicly-owned enterprises such as the Post Office and in public services such as Health. Some private businesses and professional bodies have also established Consumer Advisory Services through their industrial or professional associations.

It would seem logical to extend these advisory activities by building up consultative and representative councils in fields such as automobile repairs, hotels and catering and grocery retailing.

Parallel with the movement towards Consultative Councils we may expect a demand that the consumer interest should be represented on the boards of private companies. Public representation is already well established in government sponsored organisations in Europe. And board representation of various interests e.g. women and ethnic minorities, is a common arrangement in large US corporations, working through public responsibility committees.[6]

5. *Permanent government controls on pricing*

Opinion polls show that during a period of inflation consumers simply do not trust producers to keep their prices down. Surveys in the USA and the UK by Opinion Research Corporation indicate a dramatic shift of opinion to a position where two-thirds of the public believe that government control of prices is needed. Of course, this control has already been established on a temporary basis in the UK, and institutionalised in Price Commissions and Departments of Prices and Consumer Protection.

6. *More stringent legislation to enforce standards of safety and performance*

This already exists in legislation on car emissions and seat belts. The American Congress has also recently decided that airbags must be put into cars by 1984.

Following the thalidomide scandal, pre-testing of drugs and pesticides has reached the point where only the largest firms can afford the $10 million it now costs to launch a new product on the American market. Regulatory agencies are also liable to ask for established products to be withdrawn. This happened some time ago with DDT and currently the US Food and Drug Administration is attempting to stop the $2 billion business in saccharin and saccharin-flavoured products.

Tobacco and alcoholic drinks are two areas which may expect special attention in terms of stricter regulation of products, distribution and sales promotion.

7. *Tighter regulation of advertising and sales promotion*

Despite advertisers' efforts at self-regulation, advertising is so intrusive and the public mood so sceptical that one must anticipate continued pressure for 'literal truth' or complete disclosure in advertising.

We will almost certainly see limitations on amounts spent on promotion – a system already in use in certain parts of Europe. And, of course, we may see more controls on the use of 'wasteful' packages such as one-trip bottles and beverage cans.

8. The extension of government-sponsored consumer education and protection

Governments are already substantial advertisers, e.g. in campaigns to reduce smoking and to prevent accidents in the home and on the roads.

It is a short step from here to the setting up of Consumer Education or Consumer Protection Agencies to carry out product tests and publish the results, and to help consumers to argue their case.

Ralph Nader is currently trying to guide a Bill through the US Congress for the establishment of a federal Consumer Protection Agency with powers to intervene on behalf of consumers before federal regulatory bodies and challenge their decisions in the courts.

Management's response

How should management respond to the challenge of consumerism? There is, of course, always the possibility that business may reverse the trends but as Theodore Levitt has pointed out, 'business has not really won or had its way in connection with even a single piece of proposed regulatory or social legislation in the last three quarters of a century'.[7]

If management is to influence the development of consumer protection legislation and the activities of consumer organisations it clearly needs to devote time and resources to the task.

The specific action to be taken will vary with the size of the organisation, the reputation of the products and the risks involved. In the case of biological detergents in the USA, an erroneous rumour about their effect on the skin, started by a local doctor reduced the market share overnight from around thirty per cent to about two per cent. Ralph Nader's campaign against General Motors forced the company to withdraw a major product line. Thalidomide cost the British Distillers Company £20 million in compensation. Perhaps, the most damaging campaign of all was the series of lawsuits brought against the American General Electric Company in 1968 for price-fixing. They cost the company $250 million.

The changing role of top management

The reader may protest that the involvement of top management is the panacea offered by writers on any area from industrial relations to research and development. How can the chief executive and his board find time to become involved in every major issue? I suppose the answer must be that the chief executive becomes involved in each area sequentially, as a particular activity becomes critical to the organisation's survival and development.

Also the role of top management is changing. In a society which is increasingly seeking to control the major aspects of management decision-making, a critical function of top management must be to act as the public face of the organisation.

In the 'goldfish bowl' environment of the 1980s, companies must operate more as open systems rather than closed systems. And the open system has been described as 'the mutual permeation of an organisation and its environment'.[8]

Top management in the future will need to be capable of operating in both the older element of the market and the new elements of politics and government. To quote Conrad Voss Bark, a leading British consultant on Parliamentary affairs:

> 'The modern industrialist is much more deeply involved in the structure of society, the flux of argument about social policies and in the operation of these policies, than

he either expects or desires. His field of operation is no longer the boardroom, the market place and the shop floor. He is out in the forum as well. He may not want to take part in the debate but, if he does not, it will still go on without him. He would do better to be in than out.'[9]

Organising for consumer affairs

If top management are to act as advocates for their firms on television, in public inquiries and in discussions with representatives of consumer organisations, it may be necessary to strengthen the consumer affairs activity at the corporate level.

This may be constituted as part of a new Corporate Affairs or Public Affairs Department. In many cases the board may feel that the whole of a business's relationship with government and society needs to be put in the hands of a new department, if the company's case is to be put in a professional way.

A study by the US Conference Board in 1968 suggested that the majority of firms reviewed legislative issues continuously and a half of them made frequent representations to government, mostly to protest against government regulations when it was often too late to make substantial changes. But only five per cent of companies actually put forward constructive proposals for new legislation!

Later studies by the Conference Board have revealed that, under pressure of government legislation, 'Public Affairs is one of the newest and most rapidly developing functions as more and more firms establish formal units at headquarters level to deal with political, social and economic matters influencing their business environment'. Today threequarters of major US firms are engaged in activities which 'constitute a recognisable public affairs function'.[10]

This may require various administrative steps, for example:

1. Improving quality control and testing procedures, possibly in collaboration with the work force, to reduce consumer complaints;
2. Working with industry associations and professional bodies to raise performance standards;
3. Establishing new standards of consumer service so that this aspect of management performance is more closely monitored;
4. The use of outside consultants to check consumer attitudes to the organisation and its services;
5. Monitoring of trends in consumer organisations and in political parties, with a view to anticipating legislation;
6. The establishment of effective liaison with consumer groups e.g. by informal meetings or through joint consultative committees at various levels;
7. The auditing of present products and the tightening of performance requirements for new products, in anticipation of product liability legislation;
8. Finally, it should be possible for management to discover marketing opportunities for the organisation in the new trend towards consumerism — in 'square deal' products, open-handed advertising, 'eat by' dates on food products etc.

As a president of General Electric once said 'every management problem is a business opportunity in disguise'.

Bernard Taylor
Editor, Business and Society Series
Henley
November 1977

References

1. The Molony Committee Report on Consumer Protection, April 1962.
2. Peter Drucker, *Consumerism in Marketing*, a speech to the National Association of Manufacturers, New York, April 1969.
3. The figures quoted in this paragraph are quoted in Andrew Symington, 'Marketing in a Critical Environment' in *Management in a Changing Society*, BIM (London 1973).
4. Eirlys Roberts, 'The Impact of the Consumer Movement' in *Business Strategies for Survival*, W. D. Purdie & B. Taylor (Eds.), Heinemann (London 1976).
5. *Forbes Magazine*.
6. Michael L. Lovdal *et al*, 'Public Responsibility Committees of the Board', *Harvard Business Review*, May-June 1977, pp. 40–181.
7. Theodore Levitt, 'Why Business Always Loses', *Harvard Business Review*, Vol. 46, March/April 1968.
8. E. Trist & K. E. Emery, 'Socio-Technical Systems', *Management Sciences, Models & Techniques*, Vol. II, Pergamon Press (London 1960).
9. Conrad Voss Bark, 'Industry and Parliament, Adjusting to Social Change', *CBI Review*, 1975, p. 18.
10. *The Role of Business in Public Affairs*, 1968, p. 3 and *Organising for Effective Public Affairs*, 1969, p. 1 The Conference Board, New York.

Acknowledgements

I wish to record my gratitude to the Consumers' Association and particularly to Peter Sand, the Research Director, and David Tench, Legal Officer, for invaluable advice and help in the writing of this book. I would also like to record my thanks to Irene and Harry Chandler of the Travel Club, Upminster, Gwilym Williams of the Prestige Company Ltd., Malcolm Little of United Biscuits (UK) Ltd., Harry Shepherd of Marks and Spencer, David Sainsbury of Sainsbury Ltd., John Timpson of William Timpson and A.P. Ridley-Thompson of Boots Company Ltd. Much additional help and advice were given by the Office of Fair Trading (particularly Jeremy Mitchell, now Director of the National Consumer Council) and by J. Walter Thompson Ltd. (in particular by Stephen King). They are not, of course, responsible for any errors or omissions which are entirely the responsibility of the author.

Introduction

Consumer protection as such has a long history, going back to such mediaeval processes as the Assize of Bread, which fixed the price of the quarter loaf, and the Assize of Ale, which determined the strength of beer. It could therefore be contended with some justification that England was among the pioneers of consumer protection from the legal standpoint, particularly as the first consumer protection law, the Food and Drink Act of 1860, was enacted by the English Parliament. Also, the pioneers of the Co-operative Movement first set up in business in England and that could be regarded as the first consumer protection movement, although it did not attempt to test products or to advise its members as the founders of the consumer movement in the United States did.

The consumer movement as we know it, that is the formation of consumer societies and groups to provide information to their members about complex products, originated in the United States. These origins are given in more detail in the first two chapters of the book, but the consumer movement in all countries has not been without its opponents.

When the late Consumer Council produced its last annual report, in a funereal black cover in 1970, its Chairman, Lord Donaldson, wrote:

> I am convinced that the axing of the Consumer Council

> cannot mean the axing of what we have started. Some day someone will have to invent a new, publicly financed body to promote and protect the consumer interest.
>
> Meanwhile I fear that consumers will have to wait a long time for the fair and equitable deal in the market place that will fully satisfy the Council's expectations and aims.'

The Council had been set up after a Board of Trade Committee under the chairmanship of Mr J. T. Molony, QC, had reported in favour of the immediate establishment of a grant supported Consumer Council. In Chapter 1 an account is given of the vagaries of public policy as regards consumer protection in the years following the second world war. There can be little doubt that the abandonment of the Consumer Council after a mere seven years of existence owed something to the hostility of private enterprise.

In a letter to *The Times* six years after the demise of the Consumer Council (6 October 1976) the Vice-Chairman of the new National Consumer Council wrote:

> 'We still have a long way to go in creating a truly equitable balance between consumers and suppliers but our objectives are clear and we are on the right road.'

The theme of this book is that there is also a right road for the directors and managers of companies making and selling consumer products that this should lead them in the direction of open and fair dealing with their customers, not as a belated response to 'consumerism', but as part of a policy of social responsibility on the part of their company.

One thing is certain, and American executives are already coming to recognise this in their highly competitive economy, consumer protection of some kind is here to stay. If any manager (and it is to managers at all levels that this book is addressed) should doubt this, let him note the resolution of the Council of Europe of 14 April 1975 regarding a 'Preliminary programme of the European

Economic Community for a consumer protection and information policy'. When the resultant legislation comes into force it will affect businesses in every member country to the extent that the provider of a faulty product shall be fully liable for all damages resulting from its deficiency, *whether he was aware of it or not.* This Draconian law may be adopted by the Council next year (1978) when it has been debated by the Economic and Social Committee of the European Parliament.

The Commission has already made a community-wide survey of consumers' attitudes to advertising, a sample of 9500. 80 per cent replied that they believed that advertising is either misleading in content about quality or is designed to persuade them to buy products for which they have no real need. In short, consumers in Europe are in a critical mood and in the near future business, whether private or public, is going to have to pay more attention to them as critics and treat them less as marketing statistics.

Looking to the American scene as a harbinger of events on this side of the Atlantic, it is noteworthy that the Consumer Product Safety Act, passed about four years ago, contains provisions which authorise the Consumer Product Safety Commission to impose heavy fines (up to £50 000) and even prison sentences in serious cases for wilful violation leading to personal injury of consumers or users of a defective product. Commenting on this recent development in consumer protection in the United States a consultant, Howard Abbott, wrote in *The Times* (31 January 1977):

> 'It can be seen that the 1980s will demand a different management style from that of the 1970s. To meet the situation likely to be created by the adoption of the EEC draft directive, manufacturers are going to have to do much more than merely extend their quality control. Every product carries with it some risk.'

That may be putting it a bit too strongly, but the basic

message underlying that statement, and which is the motive for writing this book, is that managers in manufacturing and retailing in the industrialised countries of the world now need to be aware that they are confronting a new kind of market. The old Latin tag *caveat emptor* has been misunderstood in modern times and has become a watchword for the unscrupulous. It applied to the state of affairs believed to have existed in mediaeval times when the market was a physical fact and not an economist's concept.

The 'open market' or market overt was strictly controlled so that buyers were able to see and compare all the wares offered for sale. The three important offences against the law of market overt were all kinds of speculation: forestalling was the selling of goods before the market opened; regrating was buying in order to sell again rather than for consumption; and engrossing was 'cornering' particular goods in order to drive up prices. All these have been legitimate business practices for centuries and have from time to time come under fire as being against the public interest. Indeed, monopoly legislation has now become widespread although collective retail price maintenance (price rings) was not made illegal in Britain until 1956.

There remain those who, against all experience, still persist in believing in what they term free and unrestricted private enterprise. Whether they really mean wholly unrestricted is an open question for that would mean no safety legislation (every schoolboy knows how many sailors owed their lives to Plimsoll's line), no laws concerning food and drink and hygiene, no protection of the environment, no rules governing weights and measures and standards – in short commercial anarchy. This would redound to the harm of many of the enterprises involved, for most if not all firms have to buy as well as sell and, at present, they have many defences against fraud thanks to both legislation and case law.

In case it should be thought that the point under discussion is unreal, let me quote from Arthur Shenfield and Mark Green's *Business and Consumerism* (Foundation for Business Responsibility, 1972). Shenfield says that 'the consumerist sets himself up as the consumer's champion but in fact he is his enemy'. The explanation for this surprising assertion is that the establishment of 'new, better, and stricter standards of quality, safety, fitness, etc. for consumer goods ... is an assault upon the consumer, not his defence. It narrows his choice and raises costs against him'. And this author (Mr Green offers the opposite point of view) adds that 'The consumerist movement is a typical populist movement. Its roots are ignorance and discontent'. Mr Shenfield believes that the consumerist movement, like other populist causes, will fade away and businessmen will no longer have to worry about it in a few years.

The Foundation for Business Responsibility also published John Humble's *Social Responsibility Audit* the following year. It is subtitled 'A management tool for survival' and contains the view that society will increasingly and explicitly demand from business a more effective contribution to social responsibility including increased awareness that the consumer needs more not less protection, 'even where this may damage short-term profitability'. The implication must be that social responsibility is fast becoming a long-range necessity for business and that it should be built into the corporate strategy. Seen today as a short-term disadvantage, it could in ten or twenty years decide the survival of the business. That is the way the wind is blowing.

As far back as 1969 (for change is very fast nowadays) the Unilever group produced a pamphlet, *Consumer Satisfaction and Protection*, which was a reprint of the speeches to the British and Dutch annual general meetings (always held simultaneously) by Lord Cole and Mr H. S. A. Hartog, the respective chairmen at the time. They said that Unilever policy was to look for profits over the long run rather than the short, which enabled the group to offer its customers good value at low prices. 'Protecting the consumer', they went on, 'is in the interest of our business.' 'This involves considerable effort and cost but it is the price we pay to stay in business.' Whatever the individual thinks about the outcome of that policy in terms of Unilever's products and prices, this stated awareness of the importance of the customer to the company is in itself significant. Not many years ago a national airline had to circularise its staff with a reminder 'that passengers are the object of our effort and must not be regarded as an obstacle to it'. The feeling remains that too many businesses, public or private, still tend to look upon the market as a sink and not a source, in the words of Burns and Stalker.[1]

As Humble says, the consumer basically wants four rights: safety, information (open dating, for instance, in foodstuffs), a choice, and a voice. The firm which gives him or her these will command respect and attention and, who knows, perhaps loyalty. Brand loyalty is supposed to spring partly from reiterative advertising and allied point-of-sale displays and special offers. In the future we may come to find that lasting loyalty grows out of a responsible relationship with the public.

Potentially, therefore, the progressive firm (by which we mean one that leads rather than follows) stands to derive long-term material advantages from strategic marketing. These advantages will accrue in the form of a 'good image' which will be genuine and not a fabrication based solely on public relations campaigns. In addition the companies which pursue enlightened policies in their marketing and give the public a fair deal will not need to fear the tightening up of consumer protection legislation. On the contrary, they will welcome it because it will restrain the irresponsible while the responsible firms will be unaffected by it.

In 1974 the *Harvard Business Review* published in its September–October issue the results of a survey of nearly 3600 executives in United States companies who had been asked their views on the consumer movement. Many of them evidently retained their belief in consumer sovereignty, meaning that the consumer still holds the ultimate weapon of not buying a product, and that the majority of consumers have the ability to make rational buying decisions. At the same time the traditional 'buyer beware' philosophy of the market place was seen as disappearing. *Caveat emptor* is being replaced by *caveat venditor*, largely because of voluntary associations like the Consumers' Union of the United States and of federal and state legislation and regulation.

There also appeared to be a majority which supported measures to make advertising more factual and truthful. In addition, the executives felt that the most constructive approach that business could make to consumerism is to make better quality products and to treat consumer complaints with more response than hitherto. The laggard area in dealing with the consumer was seen as repair and maintenance. Finally, consumerism or consumer orientation on the part of the firm was regarded as a positive and competitive marketing tool. Consumer protection was here to stay and not a passing fad agreed 84 per cent of respondents, some of whom went as far as to assert that it must become part of corporate decision making. This last point was reinforced by the fact that 37 per cent of the executives questioned came from top and 'upper-middle' management, the decision makers.

True, that is only one survey, but it is a pointer, and quite a striking one, in the direction of the market-place of the future, in which the rational consumer, armed with information he would have lacked twenty years ago and protected by legislation which has been a century in gestation, will confront the businessman and manager across a much narrower gap of knowledge. It has often been remarked that what the consumer has lacked in recent years has been information. Worse still, he and she have been given far too much spurious, persuasive and misleading 'information' in the form of exaggerated advertising claims, deceptive packaging and the notorious 'small print' which so frequently slyly undermines a buyer's rights under the law.

It is (or should be) interesting to both consumer and supplier (and all suppliers of goods or services are consumers at some time) that firms providing an open and fair deal for customers can also be highly profitable. Among the case studies which form the third part of this book examples of such money-making paragons are given.

In the first part of the book an attempt is made to present the background to the consumer movement in the United States and Britain and latterly in the European Community. The second part is devoted to the consideration of a modern marketing strategy which embodies social responsibility.

The key to understanding the importance to the future health of business in market economies lies, in the words of the *Harvard Business Review* commenting on their survey, in the recognition and acceptance of consumerism which 'is now seen by a surprisingly large number of executives as an opportunity rather than a threat'.

References

1. *The Management of Innovation*, Tavistock, 1961.

Part 1

The genesis of consumer protection

1 The hostile environment of business

If businessmen are or have been enemies of consumer protection, their hostility has been mild compared to that of the marketing managers in their employ and of the advertising agencies employed by them in their turn. At one extreme consumer protection has been described as a first step along the path to dictatorship:

> 'If product testing led to "best buy" pronouncements, and if such pronouncements were followed by the public ... there would in effect be only one brand, one design, one type of product which a manufacturer could reasonably offer. This is a very short step indeed to the sort of control exercised for so long in the East European Socialist countries ...[1]

At the other extreme the consumer, except as a manageable buying unit, is ignored altogether. The Institute of Practitioners in Advertising published in 1968 a 'thesis', to use their own term, called *Advertising in the 21st Century* by D. S. Cowan and R. W. Jones. Admittedly it was intended to be no more than a 'model' of agency development over fifty years but nevertheless it claimed also to look at advertising objectively 'through the eyes of the manufacturer, the retailer, the media proprietor and, most refreshingly, the consumer'. In fact there is not a word about the consumer or consumerism throughout the book.

Other writers from the advertising business have decried consumerism as relatively powerless because of the small proportion of the consuming population belonging to the voluntary organisations – about one per cent in the United States and Britain. But this plain statistic leaves out of account the quality of that membership which, in Britain, has long been considered to be too upper middle-class to be truly representative. By the same token it is a highly educated, articulate and often influential membership which includes politicians, professionals of every kind, academics and 'communicators'.

It is probably because of the quality of the membership of the Consumers' Union of America and of the Consumers' Association in Britain that so much successful lobbying has been achieved in the direction of direct protection of consumers by law, as well as by the establishment of 'watchdog' committees to oversee, for example, the content of commercial television advertisements or the safety testing of pharmaceutical products.

As the self-appointed propagandists of consumer products, the advertising agencies have themselves felt and wilted under the hot breath of public criticism. In his *Shocking History of Advertising* E. S. Turner calls advertising 'the whip which hustles humanity up the road to the Better Mousetrap'. Richard Hoggart has written of 'most modern advertising as, at the best, a stupid waste of good human resources and at the worst, a wicked misuse of people'.[2] In their detailed study *The Persuasion Industry*[3] Pearson and Turner concluded that advertising people were not so much 'steely-minded manipulators of public taste' but rather 'muddled, worried men who seemed disturbingly out of touch with the very people they were paid their high salaries to convince'. And because of this isolation from the consumers they were out to persuade, advertisers were judged by Pearson and Turner to be not so much wicked as incompetent.

The debate continues, and a recent contribution which offers an exhaustive array of arguments from both sides was published in 1975 by the Advertising Association: *The Three Faces of Advertising: Ethics, Economics, Effects*, but once again the weight of opinion lies on the pro-advertising side of the balance, as one might expect in such a publication. The advertising business, hedged about as it is with comparatively new restraints, continues to be on the defensive and is unlikely to be lulled by commentators such as Robin Wight, himself an advertising executive, the very title of whose book, *The Day the Pigs Refused to be Driven to Market*, has an ominous ring to it. His coda to a lengthy excursus on advertising and the 'consumer revolution' reads as follows:[4]

> Despite all its failings, blindness, folly, ignorance and stupidity advertising still has one more chance. For the Consumer Revolution is not vengeful. It merely wishes to turn them into useful human beings.

The good old days

The above emphasis on advertising as an index to the hostile environment of business in the community shows the tip of the iceberg. The hidden depths of the berg are made up of many more factors derived from the relations between companies and their many 'publics', as the public relations writers like to put it. A contributory factor is, of course, labour relations in all its complexities and its long history of conflicts of interest.

At one time, the simple conflict of interest lay between the seller and the buyer. Economists have been at great pains in their writings to explain that a good bargain is one struck between a willing seller and a willing buyer, and one that benefits both parties. The seller makes a profit and the buyer receives goods (the word itself is expressive of satisfaction) which endow him with what the classical economists like to call 'utilities'.

This is the attractive theory. In practice the equity of the bargain will depend on the relative strengths of the bargaining position of the two parties. Traditionally it came to be realised that the seller was in a position to know more about the goods for sale than the buyer and also that the seller could take advantage of this knowledge.

The concept of market overt, ideally the completely open market with all goods displayed, fair prices or 'just prices' (sometimes decided by the local mayor) and no speculative interventions by 'middlemen' or jobbers permitted, was designed to ensure that both parties to a bargain had equal opportunities in arriving at that bargain. So carefully were city markets and country fairs controlled that it was assumed that fair trading must follow. That it seldom did in the long run was not the fault of the law makers or of the ordinary users of the markets and fairs. It was from malpractice and evasion of the common and statute laws relating to trading that public suspicion of merchants and traders originated.

The commodities generally affected between the development of the open market and its gradual erosion in the eighteenth century were food and drink and textiles. Because of the relative simplicity of knowing about such things (which country people were assumed to understand almost from childhood), the authorities were inclined to rely upon equally simple safeguards such as the Assize of Bread, which fixed the weight of a loaf at a given price, and the Assize of Ale, which kept a check upon the strength of beer, and the common law of the open market. If a buyer were to strike a bad bargain within this system it was assumed that it must be his or her own fault, hence the doctrine of *caveat emptor*.

It seems necessary to dwell briefly on this historical background to consumer protection to put in perspective the consumer movement and the law aimed at protecting consumers today, because there persists a belief or at least an opinion that a lot of modern consumer protection ought to be unnecessary. The argument seems to be that educated adults – and after all the majority of adults in industrial societies receive ten or more years of education today – should have the wisdom to make rational choices about the quality and prices of the goods they buy.

When we consider the tricks played on the buyers by market traders in the era we call early modern times – that is at the beginning of urbanisation, when variety in commodities was small and choice and judgment therefore easier than it is today – it should not surprise us that ordinary people are still apt to be misled when faced by the complex and confusing choices they have to make in the fourth quarter of the twentieth century.

When cloth was woollen, worsted or linen it could still be adulterated by mixing with inferior fibres, stretched to seem larger or not shrunk to its true dimensions. It was harder to tamper with the quality of food, but prices could be manipulated by withholding stocks (this was done, for example, at Billingsgate with fish) and there are many complaints on record of market people passing off stale produce as fresh.

With the movement of people in large numbers from country to town following the eighteenth-century enclosures and the development of factory centres, there ceased to be any control over the price and quality of goods such as had existed under the laws of the open market. As urban populations grew there was a falling off in the farming and food-producing population, a rising demand for food in the towns and a consequent temptation to increase available supplies by adulteration.

Of this development the chemist Frederick Accum wrote in his preface to the first edition of *A Treatise on the Adulterations of Food and Culinary Poisons* in 1820:

> To such perfection of ingenuity has the system of counterfeiting and adulterating various commodities arrived in this country, that spurious articles are everywhere to be found in the market, made up so skilfully as to elude the discrimination of the most experienced judges.

Two years later he reported in the fourth edition of the book that he had been threatened with uncertain penalties for his crusading work but that it would not discourage him from handing down to posterity 'the infamy which justly attached to the knaves and dishonest dealers ...'. Accum was probably the first identifiable consumerist and covered a remarkable range of malpractices from drugs and medicines, bread, beer and wine to false measures in the coal trade, although there had been previous anonymous pamphleteers who had denounced various 'tricks of the trade'.

It was largely because of Accum (who fell from grace over an accusation of mutilating books in the library of the Royal Institution – apparently he tore out end-papers on which to make notes) that the urban public became aware of the vast extent to which fraud had developed in the supply of all kinds of goods to towns and cities. As far as food was concerned many of the practices gave rise to poisoning, which was frequently fatal. It was not possible in all cases to connect cause with effect, but gradually the public and a few eminent citizens began to demand official action.

A leading campaigner was Dr Arthur Hill Hassall, who shrewdly pointed out that adulteration of taxable foodstuffs (sugar, tea, coffee, malt and many others) reduced the state revenues by as much as a tenth in addition to undermining the health and therefore the resistance to disease of growing children. It was not till 1860 that Government decided to act but its compromise measure, the Adulteration of Foods Act, was largely ineffective. It empowered local authorities to appoint a public analyst to test samples of suspect foodstuffs, but in twelve years no more than seven were appointed and only one of them, the Medical Officer of Health and Public Analyst for Dublin, ever brought any successful prosecutions or any prosecutions at all.

Years later G. K. Chesterton summed up the outrage felt by the general public in his 'Song Against Grocers':

God made the wicked Grocer
For a mystery and a sign,
That men might shun the awful shop
And go to inns to dine.

Chesterton's 'evil-hearted grocer' sold floor dust as salt, sand as sugar and crammed 'with cans of poisoned meat, The subjects of the King', but it was no joke to the people who had literally suffered from the callous indifference of the food trade. The nasty taste in the mouth lasted for generations. The trade, or 'vested interests' as such entrenched opponents of reform came to be known, kept up a strong and persistent rearguard action against reform of the law but, as Dr Burnett records,[6] even before the 1860 Act improvement in the quality of food and drink was discernible as the revelations of Dr Hassall, Dr John Postgate and the *Lancet* began to influence the more enlightened and progressive members of the trade, who were basically honest but medically ignorant.

Dr Postgate was instrumental in drafting and obtaining the passage of the 1872 Adulteration of Food, Drink and Drugs Act, which made it a criminal offence to add ingredients to foods simply to increase weight or bulk, without declaring the contents, and the sale of adulterated drugs also became a punishable offence in law. Hitherto pharmaceutical products had been outside the control of the law, although public attention had been repeatedly drawn to malpractice on the part of apothecaries, herbalists and others.

Consumers had meanwhile begun to band together to co-operate in the buying and selling of food. Of the co-operative movement of the nineteenth century, G. M. Trevelyan has said it did 'so much all over the world to stop the exploitation of the consumer by the retail dealer', and few people would accuse that particular historian of political prejudice. Among the motives behind the setting up of retail co-operatives such as the famous pioneering one in Rochdale in 1844 was the desire to avoid adulterated, stale or otherwise low-quality foodstuffs. It was a reaction by a section of the general public against the obvious malpractice of the food manufacturer and not the retailer.[7]

Not surprisingly the co-ops, as they came to be known, aroused the enmity of the other manufacturers and retailers, some of whom resented the hidden price cuts represented by the distribution of profits, the so-called dividend. Indeed some makers of famous branded goods refused to supply co-operative shops with their product. The movement grew nevertheless, at one time boasting nearly fourteen million members and handling nearly twelve per cent of the retail trade in Britain, but its constitution (hundreds of autonomous retail societies) and its system of trading (criticised by the Gaitskell Commission in 1959 for being uneconomic) gradually undermined the movement's influence over the buying public. It has since been noted that 'Recent developments in consumer protection have been mainly due to initiative from outside the Co-operative movement.'[8]

Professor Sidney Pollard argued in his book, *The Co-operatives at the Crossroads*,[9] that the consumer protection associations could not take the place of the co-operative movement because they are 'static and passive', able only to report on a sample of available goods and incapable of entering into actual production of goods of acceptable quality and performance. There is sense in this contention, but had the co-ops been able to compete with private enterprise on such terms it is arguable that there would have been no need for consumer protection of the kind that came into being in 1957 with the appearance of *Shopper's Guide*, published by the Consumer Advisory Council of the British Standards Institution, and *Which?* the journal of the newly formed Consumers' Association.

The Which? hunt

The story of the origins of the consumer protection movement has been told many times in books about the history of this collective reaction to the sale of sub-standard goods and services. Eirlys Roberts, for many years Research Director of CA, told it in some detail in her book *Consumers*,[10] beginning with the publication of *Your Money's Worth* by Stuart Chase and F. J. Schlink in 1927.

The book was based on the work of the American National Bureau of Standards which tested goods for purchase by civil government departments and by the army and navy of the United States. The authors described how the consumer in his or her ignorance could pay ten times as much for the same product as the government and two or three times as much for the products markedly inferior to those tested and bought by government agencies. They exposed to the American consumers how they were powerless to discriminate between goods of differing quality and further that the shop assistants who sold them the goods, and who were supposed to be trained in the knowledge of such goods, were equally unable to discriminate. When laboratory tests were made of household materials to rank them in order of quality, sample groups of consumers and retail assistants, using only sight, touch and whatever senses might be needed, could not duplicate the laboratory ranking. Nor were price comparisons between brands of any value in assessing quality. Chase and Schlink revealed how mail-order firms were able to supply such items as feather beds and pillows in an apparent variety of qualities at five different prices, but the only actual difference between the products was in the fancy name on the supplier's label, which was altered to fit the order.

Schlink was an engineer employed by the American Standards Association, Chase was an economist. The public response to the book, which became a best seller, was to flood them with questions about which goods to buy. The intelligent buying public had suddenly come to realise its vulnerability in the face of variety, technical complexity and sharp business practice. No doubt some American businessmen of the time would have responded to criticism of their marketing with the saying attributed to Phineas T. Barnum, the nineteenth-century showman and promoter, 'there's a sucker born every minute'.

The opposite side of that coin is that no customer likes the sensation that somebody has treated him as a sucker, which was the main motive behind the response to *Your Money's Worth*, in the form of the club founded by Schlink to advise subscribers at $1 a year, using a small testing laboratory and the techniques with which he had become familiar in his full-time work. But it was 1929, the year of the Great Crash and the resultant depression, the effect of which was to freeze the membership of Consumers' Research, or at best to permit it to grow only very slowly. In the thirties, for various reasons but chiefly because of poor pay and job insecurity, a group of Consumers' Research executives and workers hived off and founded a separate organisation which they called Consumers' Union. It grew rapidly but was not very large (70 000 members by 1939, when the war intervened two years later and once again growth slowed down), and was branded as left-wing partly because of its criticisms of manufacturers and retailers, partly because of their hostility. The organisation was cited as subversive in the twitchy years immediately before the war but was cleared of all charges before the House Un-American Activities Committee in 1952. In the post-war years, when peace-time production flooded the market once again with a confusion of brands and new products, many of which had never been seen before – ball-point pens, plastics, man-made fibres, detergents, tape-recorders, antibiotics and a hundred others – Consumers' Union grew rapidly, reaching over one million members in the sixties with their journal *Consumer Reports*.

By this time there were signs that a British consumer movement was gathering momentum. The origins of the official provision of consumer advice were complex and not unconnected with the policies of the post-war Labour administration. Beginning with Sir Stafford Cripps' Treasury Economic Information Unit and the Women's Advisory Council of the British Standards Institution, the Board of Trade eventually provided funds to found the Consumer Advisory Council and its journal *Shopper's Guide*, which began publication in 1957 under the editorship of a *News Chronicle* writer, Elizabeth Gundrey, who had already done some campaigning in that Liberal newspaper.

Almost simultaneously the sociologist, Michael Young, and a group of like-minded professionals including some lawyers and economists, launched the Consumers' Association (initially called Consumer Research but there was a consultancy firm with that name) and its journal *Which?* Eirlys Roberts, who edited the journal for many years, recalls that the biggest threat to *Which?* was thought to be the British libel laws. For one thing, manufacturers whose products were adversely criticised might bring an action for defamation against the journal, and for another, the Press in general might be wary of publicising the findings of *Which?* for fear of being involved in such an action or of losing advertising or both. There appears to have been a handful of progressive manufacturing companies whose directors privately took the view that not only would no harm result, but perhaps even some good might come of the comparative testing upon which the reports were to be based. They reasoned, with some justification, that the maker of reliable, safe and good-quality products had nothing to fear and possibly something to gain from the exposure of his inferior competitors. This was not an attitude which they were willing to make public.

There was also strong opposition to the work of the Consumers' Association on a variety of grounds. Some manufacturers felt that it was an unnecessary intrusion into the market, given that the British Standards Institution with its Kitemark seal of approval and its Consumer Advisory Council was already well established, that the founders of CA were comparative amateurs alongside companies which were household names and renowned for the high quality of their products. They argued that sample testing could be unfair because one bad example of a good product line might be bought and tested, and that the sample could never be complete because of the cost and because of the regional distribution of some goods. Some sectors of industry already had their own far from tame watchdogs, such as the textile and clothing Retail Trading-Standards Association set up in 1935. Women (to whom *Which?* was expected to appeal) already turned to the Good Housekeeping Institute for advice and looked for its seal of approval on household goods, although there were sceptics who pointed out that the parent magazine, *Good Housekeeping*, relied on advertising for a proportion of its revenue and that this might induce bias.

Martin and Smith,[11] in their study of the consumer interest, contend that CA's very independence from government, industry and any source of financial support other than its subscriptions and sale of publications brought it the confidence of the buying public. Another success factor, they add, was the publication not merely of test reports but of 'Best Buys', to which the busy housewife could turn without reading the detailed text as a guide to the purchase of appliances and other technical or otherwise complex or baffling products.

It was to these Best Buys, which at first were single choices from among the goods sampled, that many manufacturers objected. Later *Which?* published joint Best Buys and also 'good value for money' selections, partly to satisfy this criticism. But of course, in doing so, it reintroduced the element of variety and choice which the tests had been aimed at eliminating. By comparison the American *Consumer Reports* often had five or more top-ranking selections under the heading of 'Acceptable', with a much longer list of the less acceptable and a short list of those goods tested or appraised which had been found to be definitely 'Not acceptable'.

Other criticisms made by manufacturers included the impossibility of any sample being large enough in some cases to embrace all available brands (but of course behind the bewildering variety of brands there is often in reality a close resemblance of products). Also if samples were to be large enough to minimise the chance of including the odd faulty product, they would statistically have to be very large indeed and commensurately costly both to buy and to test. It was accepted by all sides to this controversy that mass-produced appliances, for example, would on occasion be defective and might have slipped through inspection, which in many industries was again carried out by random sample.

A further criticism was that *Which?* reports went out of date with design changes and technical advances and that even a monthly review could not keep up with all the alterations in all the products on the market, which would in many cases include imports. CA freely admitted this but countered with the argument that they could at least assess their members' needs and preferences and concentrate their efforts there, and this they did and still do, publishing from time to time figures showing the most constant areas of complaint by consumers. For some reason carpets headed this list for years and were also a favourable bone of contention among other consumer protection organisations including the RTSA.

Martin and Smith, under the heading of 'The Influence of Comparative Testing',[11] print the results of a few sample surveys of buyers of appliances (taken from trade journals, incidentally). These indicate that a minority of respondents to these surveys were influenced in their buying decisions by *Which?* – 9 per cent in the case of an electric cooker, 7 per cent in the case of a gas cooker – which should be a comfort to manufacturers if they feel worried by consumer reports. But they say not a word about the influence of comparative testing or any other aspect of consumer protection on marketing policies of companies making consumer goods. This is not surprising, because little or no research has been done into this question. And it is typical of publications purporting to analyse the consumer movement. The point of view of the manufacturer and retailer is seldom given.

The last annual report of the Consumers' Association available when these lines were being written gives a subscription figure for 1975–6 of over 700 000, with new members joining at an average of 2000 a week. The Director, Peter Goldman, said in his report quoted from *Money Which?* (one of four special issues: the others deal with holidays, cars and DIY):

> 'All of us must become more flexible, more willing to adapt to changing conditions, more concerned with long-term rather than short-term issues, less inclined to pin the blame on someone else ...'

As a statement about improving the British economic position it could hardly be bettered.

Nevertheless, successive British governments have vacillated wildly and unreasonably in their policies concerning consumer protection, apparently unaware that a framework of consumer protection provides solid economic benefits by reducing waste and preventing many of the losses produced by the ill effects of unscreened drugs, unhealthy food additives, dangerous household and garden chemicals – the now familiar list of what it is fashionable to label 'disbenefits'. The Molony Report[12] rightly commended the 1955 legislation contained in the Food and Drugs Act, but even that comprehensive measure could not prevent the hazards which the Safety in Medicines Committee is supposed to eliminate, and that committee came into being only as a result of public pressure for a drug screening system.

The 1962 Report of the Committee on Consumer Protection (Molony) was something of a watershed in the history of consumerism in Britain. From the inception of the voluntary consumer movement, if not before, there had existed a feeling that there ought to be some agency of government, other than the statutory offices for weights and measures and similar enforcement bodies, which could exercise greater control over the broad area of consumer goods production and distribution. Politics did not seem to play much part in the decision, following Molony's recommendation, to set up a national Consumer Council. The Council was established by a Conservative Government and 7 years later removed by a Conservative Government, which within two years had switched back to recognising once again the need for some kind of consumer affairs agency, and which evolved under successive governments of both persuasions into the present Office of Fair Trading, which looks as if it has come to stay whichever way the pendulum may swing in future.

References

1. Hobson, John W., *The Freedom of the Market Place*, Foundation for Business Responsibilities, 1974.
2. Hoggart, R., 'Where is it all leading us?', in Wilson, A., Editor, *Advertising and the Community*, Manchester University Press, 1968.
3. Pearson, J. and Turner, G., *The Persuasion Industry*, Eyre & Spottiswoode, 1965.
4. Wight, R., *The Day the Pigs Refused to be Driven to Market*, Hart-Davis, MacGibbon, 1972.
5. Davis, Dorothy, *A History of Shopping*, Routledge & Kegan Paul, 1966. Robertson, A. B., 'The Open Market in the City of London', *East London Papers*, I, 1958.
6. Burnett, John, *Plenty and Want*, Nelson, 1966.
7. Trevelyan, G. M. *British History in the Nineteenth Century and After* (1782–1919), Longmans, Green, 1937.
   Fulop, Christina, *Competition for Consumers*, Deutsch, 1964.
8. Knox, F., *Consumers and the Economy*, Harrap, 1969.
9. Pollard, S., *The Co-operatives at the Crossroads*, 1965, cited in Martin, J. and Smith G. W., *The Consumer Interest*, Pall Mall Press, 1968.
10. Roberts, Eirlys, *Consumers*, Watts, 1966.
11. Martin, J. and Smith G. W., *The Consumer Interest*, Pall Mall Press, 1968.
12. *Final Report of the Committee on Consumer Protection*, Cmnd. 1781, HMSO, July 1962.

2 A new capitalism?

The innate mistrust by the ordinary citizen of the world of business is illustrated by the persistent myths of 'everlasting' inventions, such as matches, electric lamps, nylon stockings and razor blades, bought up and suppressed by the makers of less durable equivalents for fear of being put out of business by them. Even when it is explained that long-lasting bulbs cost proportionately more to run, that the early nylon stocking was coarser and therefore tougher, that no match maker ever tried to kill the cigarette lighter and that an eternal razor blade is metallurgically impossible or at best impossibly expensive, the feeling remains that the believer regards such explanations merely as part of the sinister power of big business to manipulate the truth.

Such attitudes derive from the development of the hostile environment of business touched on in the previous chapter. That orthodox opinion has never apparently expected private enterprise to be self-disciplined is shown by the following quotation:

> 'There are unfortunately many instances where industry has found it easier to confuse, even to mislead, its customers about the terms upon which it is selling. On the other hand many companies go out of their way to be precise about the terms and conditions under which they market their product. Often it is they who prosper, usually at the expense of those companies who do not do

> so. Would that more companies saw the advantages of giving maximum information about their wares without having to be coerced into doing so first.'

The author of those lines was Mr Nicholas Ridley,[1] a Conservative Member of Parliament and at one time an Undersecretary of State for Trade and Industry. In his opinion only government can ensure that suppliers give fair measure to consumers and only government can 'police the amount ... of meat in a sausage'. An admission of moral failure on the part of enterprise which leads him on to the view that 'the "new capitalism" implies an added responsibility upon government to make the necessary regulations rather than upon industry.' An alternative view of the new capitalism, whatever that may be taken to mean, might be more appealing to businessmen themselves, especially the moral leaders hinted at in Mr Ridley's paragraph. In place of yet more control and regulation by government, a form of self-discipline by industry and commerce akin to the professional codes of conduct of doctors and lawyers, which not only lies within the competence of business as at present constituted but begins to look like an essential.

It is open to argument that if the makers and sellers of goods had resisted the temptation to take advantage of the innocence and ignorance of their customers they would not today be so hedged about with the legislation which society, in its accumulated wisdom, has seen fit to adopt. What we are now contemplating is the probability that, in the absence of proper codes of conduct accepted by private entrepreneurs in the interests of the future of enterprise, we shall see a steady and inexorable increase in constraints. If there is to be a new capitalism it has to come from the capitalists and not from the state. That is the thesis. And the antithesis is that unless it does originate from business itself then business must expect to have it imposed willy-nilly.

If it could be proved that 'good ethics is good business' – a sentiment voiced by one of the entrepreneurs interviewed for the illustrative case histories which appear in Part III – then no doubt many more companies would modify their marketing strategies to take the long-run advantages promised implicitly by that policy. Unfortunately there is nothing in the way of a general proof that fair trading and consumer orientation, social marketing as opposed to hard selling, offers an invariable advantage over the less scrupulous competitor. Indeed, in the short run the competitive advantage probably goes to the sharp practitioner rather than to the fair dealer. In the short run it pays to skip or limit quality control. In the long run poor quality leads to falling sales.

The most that can be done, without an elaborate survey which might not be conclusive, is to say that a consumer-oriented marketing policy does not seem to have harmed the companies who adopted it, but rather it seems that those progressive companies have consistently shown good results (as the cases in Part III confirm).

The American Motor Corporation is a relative newcomer to the automotive market of the United States, and faced competition from three big and well-established groups: General Motors, who held over half the market, Ford and Chrysler. In 1972 American Motors had acquired 2.7 per cent of the domestic car market in the United States. In that year they introduced a Buyer Protection Plan. Working on the realisation that assembly-line car production does not make for 100 per cent fault-free output, the company decided to 'stand behind the product' by accepting unconditionally their responsibility for all defects under warranty. In place of the suspicious and reluctant attitude of car dealers and makers in the face of customer complaints about new cars, American Motors undertakes to do all repairs to their cars (those which can be shown to be due to faulty materials or workmanship) free of charge to the customer, and at the works not at the dealers. Two years after the introduction of the Plan, American Motors was able to claim 4.7 per cent of the car market, an increase of 75 per cent. Not great shares, but remarkable in the tough competitive conditions of the United States automobile industry.

A vice-president of the company, John C. Secrest, writing in Jones and Gardner's *Consumerism: A New Force in Society* [2] says:

> 'The matter of consumerism ... is something business leaders must face squarely – not for altruistic reasons, but because the well-being of our companies and our competitive enterprise system depends on it.'

In contrast to the attitudes taken by the larger automobile companies, as indicated in Ralph Nader's *Unsafe At Any Speed* [3] and Graham Turner's *The Car Makers* [4] for Britain, this looks like a great step forward. However, it cannot be taken to follow automatically that American Motors will continue to increase its market share to a level which might be thought to threaten the big three, because in the long run they, too, will have to pay more attention to the market.

Some evidence that there are marketing benefits to be gained from a pro-consumer sales policy in the car industry appear in Robertson,[5] *The Lessons of Failure*. Using statistics assembled by the Consumers' Association in a survey of 30 000 car-owning members he showed that British cars (or British made) had the highest 'time off road' record in the years 1966–9, the leading offender in most years being Vauxhall, and that the same company had the highest record of breakdowns on journeys in the same period. As Turner demonstrates in *The Car Makers*,[4] there is little quality control or inspection in the British car industry, although this is contested in an appendix by a manufacturer, who maintains that quality cannot be put into a product by means of inspection, 'if the quality is not there to start with', and goes on to assert that the quality of British cars was increasing (in 1962–3) while that of Continental makes was declining.

In view of what happened to the British domestic market in the decade which followed the publication of Turner's book, one has to conclude that that manufacturer was indulging in wishful thinking. By 1968 foreign cars had captured 8 per cent of the home market, by 1973 they had raised their share to over 20 per cent, and last year (1977) it threatened to rise to 50 per cent. What explanation can there be for such a dramatic movement away from British built motor cars in the sixties and seventies? The most likely explanation must lie in delivery dates and quality and reliability, no matter what the industry itself says, even if part of the blame (as it emerges from Turner's Chapter 5, 'Why the Quality of our Cars Suffers') must rest with the attitudes of assembly line operatives, who, for a variety of reasons, some of them not attributable to 'bloody-mindedness', skimp their work and resent inspection (which may lead to rejection) as a threat to their earnings when on piece rates.

The main point about the car industry, which is why it has been made central to this argument, is that it has serious technical problems because of the complexity of the product, but also because of the cost of that product to the consumer it comes under sharper criticism than most other consumer goods industries. Nevertheless it is a mistake for management in the automobile industry to take refuge from such criticism in evasions of responsibility and in counter-attacks on the consumer organisations (even the Automobile Association, in its magazine *Drive*, had to say that in the small car market Fiat and Renault were replacing British makes, in particular the Vauxhall Viva, because of poor finish and unreliability). And it takes a long time (10 or 15 years in the case of the British car industry) for the full impact of the consumer's silent protest to reveal itself. The heavy losses of the British car firms in recent years must in part have been brought about by their falling market shares at home, and not only by poor labour relations, which is the standard explanation.

A similar situation, without the obvious labour-management disputes to distract attention, exists in the United States. Nader[3] records that *Consumer Reports*, the journal of the Consumers' Union, reported that in 1965 the quality of American automobiles which they had bought for test, had fallen 'to new depths of shoddy workmanship'. The condition of the sample cars 'so far as sloppiness in production goes, in the whole ten-year stretch of deterioration which began in 1955, the first year in which US car sales first approached eight million' was about the worst they had experienced. So perhaps we should not be too surprised at the quiet success of America's smallest automobile manufacturer.

The manufacturer, whether of cars or any other product, has often found in the past an uncritical consuming public. As standards of living have risen and enabled the consumer to obtain new products of which he or she had never even dreamed (but which had been in the possession of the better off for some years), the satisfaction engendered by mere possession was probably enough to offset any dissatisfaction experienced with the product. Also these new products, wireless sets or radios, vacuum or suction cleaners or carpet sweepers, rayon stockings and underwear for the ladies, acoustic gramophones powered by clockwork, fountain pens, to nominate a handful that began to spread in the Britain of the 1930s, were not expected to exhibit fault-free performance. Their proud owners were largely content to possess them as indications of self-advancement. Ambitious seeking after more and better possessions came with the development of what are now termed 'the media', with their tendency (as a group of communication channels of a most vivid kind – the cinema, radio, television) to glorify the latest fad, most likely American, from grapefruit and the vitamin craze to streamlined limousines and private swimming pools.

It is not surprising that what Kotler[6] has called the 'consumer flare-ups' first took place in the country where the trend towards increasing ownership of complex and technical products was earliest and most marked, the United States of America. Kotler notes three such periods of consumer agitation, in the 1900s, the 1930s and the 1960s. The first of these seems in part to have been triggered off by those evangelising authors and journalists known as the 'muck-rakers', the most notable and best remembered of them probably being Upton Sinclair, author of *The Jungle*, a novel highly critical of the Chicago meat packing industry, and which was partly responsible for the passing of the 1906 Meat Inspection Act. It was the activity of writers like Sinclair which led to legislation such as the Pure Food and Drugs Act, 1906, and the eventual establishment of the Federal Trade Commission in 1914. These were the early results of what Kotler cogently describes as the 'strained relations between standard business practices and long-run consumer interests.' It is interesting and significant to see that phrase 'standard business practices', because in the last quarter of the twentieth century it is easy to forget that what was once standard practice can now be a crime.

The catalogue of anti-consumer offences on the part of business, past and present, is long and varied. Professor Will Straver of the Fontainebleau management centre INSEAD, in a paper on the international consumerist movement,[7] has classified them. Products are too many in number and too similar, said to be new when they are not ('false innovation'), artificially differentiated, sometimes useless and sometimes dangerous or defective. Packages are sometimes deceitful, unnecessarily expensive, inadequately labelled, undated in the case of perishables, or lacking in user instructions. Also, since the advent of plastics, the packages themselves can be pollutants. Pricing is confusing, misleading (4p off, but no base price), maintained by agreement (now illegal in most countries), unrelated to quality, related to unreasonably high profit margins, unrelated to quantity or related to fictitious promotions. Distribution has deceitful promotions, hard selling methods tied to deceitful 'special offers', poor after-sales service and sometimes none at all, misleading credit terms and the pretence of apparently high added value which in reality is just a price increase and a marginal design change. On the communication side business manipulates customers, creates superfluous needs, makes false claims, contributes to inflation (always hotly denied), promotes planned obsolescence and discontent, gives society false values and, in short, sets a thoroughly bad example in terms of truth telling, moral behaviour and honest dealing. The charge sheet appears as Table 2 in Professor Straver's paper and here we have made room for only a fraction of it.

We have seen in Chapter 1 how one reaction to the evident lack of value for money in a wide range of United States products in the 1930s was the book *Your Money's Worth* by Chase and Schlink, followed by the establishment of, among other, the Consumers' Union of America. This was part of Kotler's second consumer flare-up, attributable he thinks to high prices. The Great Crash on Wall Street must also have sharpened criticism of the 'system', but the development of the consumer movement was interrupted by the outbreak of war in 1941 (when the United States joined the Allies after Pearl Harbor).

The third and most important flare-up came well after the war and soon after the American movement had communicated itself to Britain in the late 1950s, particularly with the setting up of the Consumers' Association by Michael Young (see Chapter 1). It was set off by the arrival on the scene of Ralph Nader with his attack on the safety of automobiles in *Unsafe at Any Speed*, and the campaign waged against him in return by General Motors, who by all accounts did themselves no good at all by this behaviour. Indeed, one is tempted to add that this aggressive and somewhat sinister reaction (the company tried by probing Nader's private life to throw mistrust and suspicion upon him) had the opposite effect from what had been intended. Instead of putting Nader down, GM succeeded in giving him more publicity than he might otherwise have had, with the result that he rapidly built up a public following and a reputation as a crusader.

Kotler, however, contends that Nader was only one of many factors in the 1960s consumer flare-up, and that another and most important one was the various scandals about ethical drugs, thalidomide being the outstanding example. Well before the full story of that tragic mistake became public, there had been the Hearings on Administered Prices before the Subcommittee on Antitrust and Monopoly of the Committees of the Judiciary, US Senate. The drugs inquiry, in front of Senator Estes Kefauver and others, ran for two years, 1959–61. He gives his own account of the proceedings and their consequences in his book *In a Few Hands*.[8] Remarkably, the Drug Industry Antitrust Act was passed by 1962. Yet five years later Dr Richard Burack of Harvard Medical School was compelled in his *Handbook of Prescription Drugs*[9] to demonstrate that the American public was still being persuaded to pay unnecessarily high prices for ethical drugs when much cheaper equivalents were freely available to their medical advisers on prescription. Anticipating the standard objection that the substitutes are generally inferior in some way to much publicised and promoted brand leaders, Dr Burack observes that 'no single patient of mine who has been treated with a generic-equivalent drug has experienced anything but the effect which could be expected'. A pharmaceutical manufacturer giving evidence to the Senate Hearings is on record as saying 'the public does not benefit from the applied research of the pharmaceutical industry. It is also obvious that the selling price for a particular ethical specialty product is not predicated on the cost of the materials but, rather, predicated on what the traffic will bear.'

There were many other factors at work in the 1960s and some of them are still in existence. More widespread higher education produces alert and critical people with higher incomes and in some cases an enhanced sense of civic responsibility. Inflation, partly caused by two controversial colonial-style wars in the case of the United States, racial stresses, environmental anxieties, the unresponsiveness of most politicians and an increased awareness of unscrupulous marketing practices all contributed to a form of social tension which manifested itself in crusades such as Nader's 'raiders', the environmentalists and consumerism in general. Business was under heavy fire and facing growing criticism leading to restrictive legislation – Truth-in-Lending, Truth-in-Packaging, Auto Safety, the Office of Consumer Affairs, the Environmental Protection Agency, and a greatly strengthened Food and Drugs Administration and Federal Trades Commission.

On the grounds that because business failed to discipline itself and therefore had in the end to be disciplined by the state, it is arguable that, as Kotler avers, a strong consumer movement with legislation in mind was inevitable. He also suggests that under present conditions it will continue and grow, and draws a parallel with the labour movement, that it is beneficial to the economy in the long run, being anti-waste, that it is leading to a refinement of the marketing concept, but, most important of all for business, *it can be profitable*. He recognises that the majority of entrepreneurs will disagree with these opinions. They are accustomed to thinking in quite the opposite way, partly because until recently the balance of power has always lain with the seller, who can produce what he likes at whatever price he decides and promote it on any scale, subject nowadays to the constraints of various national laws on misdescription and deception. But at one time there were no such constraints.

This trial of strength is new, for only within the last twenty years has the consumer been able to exhibit any sinews and use them, but the clash of opposed attitudes is as old as *caveat emptor*, a doctrine which we have seen is acceptable and workable only as far as the law and custom of society compel the producer and the merchant to obey the rules. In mediaeval England it was the civic authorities, drawn from the ranks of tradesmen, and the guilds of trades who regulated the commercial behaviour of citizens. Modern society may gradually be returning in a roundabout way to self-discipline by business, as a more pleasant alternative to close discipline, perhaps accompanied by increasingly heavy penalties, by the state.

The future of industrial economies is beginning to pivot on long-run welfare considerations rather than on short-term satisfactions. Short-term satisfactions bring built-in obsolescence with them and therefore waste of resources. Today's petroleum becomes tomorrow's dumps of unusable plastic waste, part of an irreversible process of destroyed resources. Admittedly the average consumer does not, or did not, give much thought to the forests cut down to provide his daily scandal sheet, to the depopulation of the oceans to provide fish fingers and pet food, to air pollution, water contamination and environmental damage in general. These concerns are expressed and discussed and sometimes campaigned about by a comparative minority. But it is not, or should no longer be, the attitude of business that because the average consumer is ignorant and insensitive it is 'standard practice' to exploit that ignorance and take advantage of that insensitivity by being just as thoughtless in return.

It is, therefore, encouraging to note that some businesses are beginning to lead the way to a situation where long-term utilities, safe and healthy products which give lasting pleasure and satisfaction, take the place of immediately desirable but defective or even dangerous products marketed with an eye to quick and profitable sales. A selection of British companies pursuing enlightened policies profitably is given in Part III. We have seen how the American Motor Corporation has made headway against the giant corporations. From Philip Kotler's article[6] and another by Aaker and Day[10] we have the following American examples dating from the 1960s, so that we might expect the trend to have increased.

Whirlpool Corporation, makers of domestic appliances, have a free complaints service and improved warranties giving the buyer more protection from defective products. A vice-president of the company, reporting greatly increased sales, which had subsequently grown at three times the average in the industry, added, 'Our interest in the consumer has to be one of the reasons'.

Giant Foods, a very large supermarket chain in Washington, DC, introduced unit pricing, open dating, nutritional labelling and refused to stock deceptive packs. They accepted that benefits might be indirect and that any pay-off might be deferred beyond their accustomed rate of return, but were able to report increased goodwill, leading to increases in sales.

Other pioneers appear to be Sears with a phosphate-free detergent (there are other, smaller firms in the US making biodegradable detergents from organic compounds other than petroleum-based raw materials), Pepsi-Cola with a biodegradable plastic bottle, Quaker Oats with new breakfast cereals based on nutrients and vitamins, oil companies such as American and Mobil with low-lead or lead-free motor spirit and Hunt-Wesson Foods who no longer advertise minor product changes at all let alone calling them 'new' and 'improved' which had become 'standard practice' in the consumer goods industries.

Commenting on these pro-consumer activities and

policies Aaker and Day remark: '... a posture of resistance, coupled with purely defensive programs, is likely to be counter-productive in the long-run because it increases the probability of government regulation with all the attendant problems of inflexibility, high costs, and new inequities created by unworkable rules and uneven administration'. This is the situation which industrial societies are beginning to face and to which business is beginning to adjust, albeit slowly and reluctantly, because there is a strong residual feeling that the consumer movement may yet lose its influence and fizzle out.

Even if this were likely (and the signs and portents are that it is highly *un*likely) it does not seem probable that governmental consumer protection policies will go sharply into reverse. What is more likely to happen is that, as and when the consumer goods and service industries adopt policies favourable to the consumer, the pressure from government agencies will naturally decrease and further legislation will progressively become unnecessary. But at present rates it looks like taking a long time. Such a change of attitude and action would, however, be a giant stride in the direction of a 'new capitalism' which might do more for private enterprise than any amount of subscribing to political parties and public relations agencies.

It is not so much dishonesty that is under fire from the consumerists – what one may term straightforward underhand dealing is bound to be short-term and unrewarding, if not the primrose path to the bankruptcy court. It is the short-sightedness of manufacturers and retailers that the consumer movement has in its sights. An exemplary segment of big business now leads the way towards what we may, with justification, describe as a 'new capitalism', under the general banner of business responsibility, having a much broader programme, with its emphasis on the environment and what it has become fashionable to call the 'quality of life'. But surely the foundation for a good, lasting and profitable business, of any size, is the customer's confidence deriving from a well-founded belief that each transaction he or she makes will bring satisfaction, and does not need to be the opening skirmish in the age-old battle between the makers and the users.

You would think so, until you listen to the comments of some quite important businessmen (whose wives in all probability have a jaundiced view of 'the market', in spite of their high purchasing power). No names, no pack-drill (or writs), but one company chairman is on record as saying that 'we need to watch the watchers' who tend to glory in 'manufacturer bashing' for its own sake, although to give him his due he did add that 'bureaucracy needs criticism to keep in touch with people's needs ...'. Obviously he is suspicious that consumer protection is a quasi-political bandwagon on which the politically ambitious may leap for the sake of the impetus. The rising tide of opinion is providing an early warning that responsible marketing must be the style of the near future, if your business is to survive – and prosper.

References

1. Ridley, Nicholas, M.P., *The New Capitalism*, Foundation for Business Responsibilities, 1974.
2. Jones, M. G. and Gardner D. M., *Consumerism; A New Force in Society*, D. C. Heath, 1976.
3. Nader, Ralph, *Unsafe at Any Speed*, Grossman, 1965.
4. Turner, Graham, *The Car Makers*, Eyre & Spottiswoode, 1963.
5. Robertson, Andrew, *The Lessons of Failure*, Macdonald, 1974.
6. Kotler, Philip, 'What Consumerism Means for Marketers', *Harvard Business Review*, May–June 1972.

7. Straver, Will, 'The International Consumer Movement: Theory and Practical Implications for Marketing Strategy'. Paper given at INSEAD, Fontainebleau, October 1976.
8. Kefauver, Estes, *In a Few Hands: Monopoly Power in America*, Penguin, 1966.
9. Burack, J., *A Handbook of Prescription Drugs*, Random House, 1967.
10. Aaker, D. A. and Day G. S., 'Corporate Responses to Consumerism Pressures,' *Harvard Business Review*, Nov–Dec 1972. See also Weiss, E. B., 'Marketers Fiddle While Consumers Burn,' *Harvard Business Review*, July–August 1968.

3 The legal background

It is not uncommon to hear from businessmen and managers today the complaint that the consumer is now 'over protected', by which they appear to mean that the laws protecting the consumer are now much more comprehensive and more strictly enforced than even ten years ago.

Policy has wavered in most countries as to how far governments should go in protecting the consumer by law. As we have seen, it was relatively simple to establish a few rules of conduct between buyer and seller in the days when the main goods bought and sold were foodstuffs and textiles, and for the most part these were also few in their variety, and quality was more easily perceived. The impact of technology as it developed in the past century and a half changed all that.

As we have seen earlier (Chapter 1) the first and most vociferous objections to underhand selling methods concerned the adulteration of food and drink, but the resultant legislation, which took many years to reach the statute book (the British were first with consumer protection law, as they were first with the social changes which engendered it) was both feeble and without any enforcement system to back it up. The early factory acts, aimed at improving working conditions and safety in

British industry, were virtually useless until a force of inspectors was recruited, and then there were no more than four for the whole kingdom! It has nearly always been difficult to pass and enforce laws which cramp the style of influential groups, such as factory owners and manufacturers.

There is nothing particularly sinister about this fact, that pressure groups shape the laws of a land. On reflection there appears to be no other way in which a society arrives at a point where it operates according to a set of rules, written or unwritten. And while it may be true that there is in some societies one law for the poor and another for the rich, the 'poor' – that is the majority of people in a society who do not command more than a minority of the resources – eventually redress the balance by using the method of pressure groups, whether these be trade unions, cooperative trading societies or consumer protection associations. The most influential pressure groups at present in our society are: the political parties, with their direct access to members of Parliament; the Trades Union Congress, which came to be recognised as being of importance to government during the Second World War; and the Confederation of British Industries, the spokesman for a large segment of industrial employers and as counterbalance to the TUC and its constituent unions. (For a general discussion of pressure groups and their relation to Parliament, readers are referred to J. D. Stewart's *British Pressure Groups*, Clarendon Press, Oxford 1958).

Yet this fifth estate, as Stewart dubs pressure groups, has so far not extended itself at the national level to include a group which speaks for consumers, although Dr Michael Young evidently believes that the National Consumer Council, which he was instrumental in founding, should be able or should be enabled to play that part.* Hitherto it has seemed that national representation of interests polarises around the property owners and employers of labour at one extreme and around the wage and salary earning employed who own little if any property at the other. All these individuals which constitute these groups are consumers, and this may have been one reason for the slowness of either broad interest group to become aware of consumers as another interest group.

There are, of course, many other interest groups which do not pursue what we may describe as 'economic' interests. They have non-economic cultural or social goals, such as clean air, road safety, the abolition of cruelty to children or animals (such groups try to represent the interests of those unable to represent themselves), and in doing so frequently clash with the economic interests of other groups. The environmentalists and the consumerists are two such broad groups. If their desires are to be met the cost of production is sure to increase in some way, or there will be some other erosion of profit margins.

Resale price maintenance offers a clear-cut example of opposing interests of business and the consumer, and at the same time is an outstanding instance of business practice which ran counter to the established doctrine of *laissez-faire*. It is the proponents of *laissez-faire*, sometimes defined as the belief or tenet that government should not interfere in economic affairs, but also more widely that enterprise should not be restricted in any way. Those who hold these beliefs should, logically, object to systems such as resale price maintenance (r.p.m.) because they enable the manufacturer to enforce prices upon the retailer of his goods. One defence of r.p.m., by the individual manufacturer as opposed to a price-fixing cartel, was that it

---

* As a result of campaigning and lobbying, mainly by CA, we now have a Department of State for Prices and Consumer Protection, the Office of Fair Trading, the Trade Descriptions Act 1968, Supply of Goods (Implied Terms) Act 1973, Consumer Credit Act 1974, Unsolicited Goods and Services Act 1971, Litigants in Person (Costs and Expenses) Act 1975, Unfair Contract Terms Act 1977 and a strong move to change the Common Agricultural Policy into a common food policy.

gave the consumer the convenience of knowing that his favourite brand was always sold at a uniform price in all shops and stores, whereas had the manufacturer permitted price-cutting the would-be purchaser would waste time and energy 'shopping around'. Allied to the branding and advertising of goods, manufacturers looked upon r.p.m. as a useful marketing tool, which also gave them the advantage of being able to forecast sales revenue more accurately than if prices were to be fixed freely by market forces.

An economist[1] renowned in the 1950s for his assault on r.p.m. wrote of it as 'one of several developments in industry and trade which have operated against the interests of consumers'. In his view, r.p.m. was one of several such developments which had caused 'the subordination of the interests of consumers to those of producers (public and private)' and that the time had come – the date was 1954 – to set about reversing the trend. This piece of pressure group activity was to a certain extent led by economists (such as the group who founded and wrote for the Institute of Economic Affairs, a body dedicated to the enfranchisement of enterprise) and was eventually successful in the passing by Parliament of the 1956 Restrictive Trade Practices Act, which outlawed collective price fixing, and the 1964 Resale Prices Act, which forbade suppliers from fixing minimum prices for customers and using the threat of withdrawing of supplies as a sanction.

Various texts on the subject (such as Pickering,[2] or Wilberforce, Campbell and Elles[3] on the legal aspects) give the impression that common law had for a long time been against price fixing as being in restraint of trade, and therefore counter to the ideal of *laissez-faire*, but that over the years the courts and the accumulation of case law had tended to be in favour of the suppliers and not the consumer. Pickering also suggests that it was in the retail trade that price maintenance first began to break down and

McClelland[4] reinforces this belief, writing as a retailer as well as an economist. And Knox[5] quotes a director of a supermarket chain, interviewed by a trade paper in 1952, as saying that the time had come for the customer to be offered price advantages, not merely convenience (self-service) and novelty, adding that the first cracks in the price structure appeared in 'safe' lines which did not bring the retailers into conflict with their suppliers under the r.p.m. rules. It took the law to make price competition available right across the retail trade.

The case of resale price maintenance is one of advantage accruing to consumers because of opposed interests in the world of business, but most of the other gains made by consumers as regards protection by law from a variety of business practices have been made recently and by means of pressure applied by interest groups, following the Galbraithian concept of countervailing power as outlined in his book *American Capitalism*.[6]

Until a few years ago it was common to hear the argument that consumers had only to withdraw their patronage for business to respond and to remedy defective products. That may be so, but it takes only a second's thought to realise what a lengthy process such a gradual decline in popularity must be. The argument also rests on the assumption of free competition which provides the consumer with easily accessible alternatives. It allows no place for the monopolist in the scheme of things and there is a great deal of monopolisation of leading products in industrialised countries, as the numerous studies of the Monopolies Commission demonstrate. Petrol, tyres, detergents, tobacco, beer, infant milk foods, electric lamps have all been scrutinised, and there are several other important groups of commodities provided by one firm or a handful of large companies, which renders the concept of 'consumer sovereignty' or of a 'consumers' strike' rather idealistic (an American professor, Mario Pei, did outline the nature of a consumers' strike in his Consumers' Manifesto[7]).

There have arisen as counterbalances, therefore, two means of strengthening the consumer against the producer and the retailer. One is the protection of being well-informed about products and conditions of sale, the other is the protection of the law, one branch of which aims to ensure that the information is true and accurate. As we have seen, the more responsible company, which also appears to be the better marketing company, gives such information to its customers and thus earns their goodwill, trust and continuing support. But there are more companies that do not follow such exemplary policies and it is for their sake that the body of consumer law has been developed. These are not necessarily fraudulent firms. The Sale of Goods Act, 1893, as interpreted by Fridman[8] makes specific mention of 'innocent misrepresentation'. It is instructive to look at the mass of litigation arising from that particular Act during seventy years of its existence (Fridman's book came out in 1966, long before the amendment of the original Act by the Supply of Goods (Implied Terms) Act in 1973.) A buyer who was in some way dissatisfied by goods purchased from a retailer could have had recourse to civil law against the seller, the act of purchase being a form of contract between the parties concerned. Naturally civil actions generally took place when the transaction involved was an important one in money terms, and probably also where the buyer was both knowledgeable and with access to legal advice.

The older statute was intended to ensure that an article bought must comply with any description accorded it by the seller or by the buyer (if the seller responded to his description by offering an article for sale) or by the manufacturer on a label or a package, or orally by a shop assistant during the sale. Similarly, if a product purchased as capable of doing a certain job – receiving radio signals, cutting wood, making toast or whatever its implied function might be – and it could not, then under the Act it would be deemed to be not what the seller suggested it was, and the buyer would have a claim. Put like that it was easy to perceive why the Act was in need of amendment, but that amendment was eighty years in the making. The three essentials (compliance with description, fitness for purpose and merchantability) were there in 1893, but the 1973 Act tidied them up.

Now, according to the Office of Fair Trading's leaflet *Fair Deal*, the seller has three obligations under the amended statute: he has to stand by the merchantable quality of the goods (that is, they must be edible, wearable, usable in the manner promised); he must sell goods that are 'fit for purpose' (a bucket must not leak, for example); and the goods must answer to the description given to them (a gaudy illustration of, say, a packed fruit pie on its wrapper must not belie the pie's contents). The major change from the 1973 Act was to prevent sellers depriving by 'small print' buyers of the rights the 1893 Act gave them. The Act empowers the consumer to return unsatisfactory goods and receive full recompense in cash – *not* a credit note – a policy already adopted by a few progressive firms. An exchange or a repair may be accepted by the customer at his or her discretion. The full responsibility for customer satisfaction lies upon the seller under present legislation, which is why more retail groups are beginning to set up testing houses. The law does not apply in the case of private sales or of sales of used goods unless the seller says or writes something misleading about the quality or condition of the goods, but that might possibly lead to a prosecution under the terms of the Trade Descriptions Act, which has replaced and superseded the 1887 Merchandise Marks Act.

This earlier Act was concerned with the accuracy of labelling in the case of number, quantity, measure, weight or gauge of goods, or the country or place of manufacture, the method of manufacture and many other characteristics.

Both Acts provided for civil proceedings on the customer's part if she or he had genuine cause for dissatisfaction and the seller had not made good the defects, replaced the article or refunded the money. If the buyer has examined the goods, seen a possible defect and still accepted them, he has no grounds for action, but under the Powers of Criminal Courts Act s.35 the criminal court may award compensation to the victim. Under the old statute, an article accepted immediately became the buyer's property, unless he objected to a fault on the spot. Afterwards he was not entitled to return it, but retailers were not always aware of the niceties and details of existing law that might affect them.

The situation has changed radically under the Trade Descriptions Act, 1968, because inaccurate description of goods or services for sale has been made a criminal offence. In Case Study 1, *the Travel Club*, will be found the cautionary tale of a transparently honest tour operator who had to spend a lot of time and a large sum of his own money combating a charge under this draconian Act that his brochure contained misdescriptions, such as the 'villa being walking distance from the sea'. He had rightly refused to plead guilty, which is usually the suggestion made in these circumstances by local trading standards offices so that prosecution can be quick and economical. The OFT leaflet, in giving a brief layman's description of the Act, noted that in the case of service industries, such as travel, a trader can be prosecuted only if his description is knowingly or carelessly given inaccurately. Presumption of innocence may be accepted in the case of service industries, but less so in the sale of goods. Although liability is strict, there are defences which may be admitted under the Act.

The same Act outlaws false pricing, such as one used to see in some sales, with a crossed out price and the new price side by side. The deleted price must have been the actual price of the article for at least twenty-eight consecutive days in the preceding six months. Another offence under the Act is to claim that prices are lower than they really are, but the Act does not appear to catch the unpriced article marked 'fourpence off', but the Office of Fair Trading has plans to make orders under the Fair Trading Act of 1973.

The trading standards officers of local authorities enforce this law and they are empowered to enter premises, inspect goods and seize them if they have need to examine or analyse them on behalf of the public. When a prosecution against a trader succeeds in England or Wales, courts have the authority to award the complainants compensation in addition to any fines or costs they impose on the accused. In England and Wales it is this Act more than any other which may be considered to have given meaning to *caveat venditor*, let the seller beware. The Office of Fair Trading appear to be encouraging customers to meet their local advisory officers to obtain help in the preparation of cases against traders. Their leaflet *Fair Deal* says, 'If you want to prepare your own individual complaint against the trader you can do so ...' and goes on to offer more information in a section called 'Going to Law', including the possibility of obtaining legal aid and adding that the Lord Chancellor's Office publishes two booklets to help litigants, *Suing on Your Own* and *Small Claims in the County Court* both by Michael Birks.

In the next few years membership of the European Community may mean that trade descriptions will have to be 'harmonised' among the constituent countries. In Case Study 4 can be found an example of the conflict of traditional generic names for kinds of biscuit – which are not literally true, there being no cream in a 'cream cracker' – but English people know that and know precisely what product to expect under that name. More seriously, there has been strong critism of 'ice cream', which contains no actual cream, but is made in this country, with milk powder (MSNF, meaning milk solids not fat). For the future, manufacturers will have to think deeply about the nomenclature adopted for their products to ensure that they are not unintentionally infringing the law.

This increasing stringency of consumer protection seems to proceed from the impetus given to the movement towards fair trading started by questionable manufacturing and trading practices such as have been described earlier: food and drink adulteration, false claims for drugs and other products, false weights and measures. And it should not be supposed that such unethical behaviour has now been completely eliminated from British business. There may well be apparent justification for using packaging which makes the contents appear greater than they are – for instance, the false walls and bottom of a face cream jar may not be present solely to deceive the customer optically into thinking that she is buying more than the maker is providing, but also to be eye catching as a container among many others on a shelf in a chemist's shop. The customer, under the general provisions of the weights and measures legislation, is protected from misleading packaging because many of the items she buys ready packed have to be marked with the amount of the contents, and from 1978 in the European Community such an amount will have to be stated in metric terms. Some companies are already putting metric measures on their packs alongside the more familiar pounds and ounces, or feet and inches, or pints or fluid ounces.

The 1963 Weights and Measures Act actually says under Section 24(1) that an offence shall have been committed if 'any person who, in selling or purporting to sell any goods by weight or other measurement or by number, delivers or caused to be delivered to the buyer a lesser quantity than that purported to be sold or than corresponds with the price charged ...' There are, of course, many consumer goods not sold by stated measure, which free the producer of the necessity to mark a weight, length or number or any other measure on the item or its container. But it does seem that there is pressure to bring as many goods in under the weights and measures legislation as possible. The thinking here seems to be that, especially in terms of acute inflation, there is a temptation for the producer to make hidden price changes by adjusting the amount sold at a given price.

The original intention of a national Weights and Measures Statute when the first Act became law in 1878 was to bring some uniformity into the measures used by traders. As Borrie and Diamond[9] say the intention was 'to establish national standards: to ensure that a pint of ale was the same in York as it was in London'. That had also been the intention of Magna Carta, but until the nineteenth century it had not been possible to set up and operate a nationwide system of control and enforcement by inspectors. These weights and measures inspectors have now become trading standards inspectors and their powers have been substantially increased. They also have to pass quite stiff qualifying examinations.

The consequences for manufacturers and retailers are serious. When what are known commonly as 'pre-packed' goods are sold and the weight has to be marked by law, inaccuracy over the marked weight cuts into profit margins, and inaccuracy under the marked weight can lead to prosecution. The quarterly reports of the trading standards inspectors reveal how numerous offences are under this Act, many of them arising from carelessness rather than deliberate fraud. The innovation and application of highly accurate measuring instruments such as the electronic check-weigher, have enabled producers to avoid the costly business of overweight and the risk of underweight.

Foodstuffs and pharmaceuticals, as their processors and producers know all too well, carry additional statutory protection for the consumer under the Food and Drugs Act of 1955, which makes it a criminal offence to sell food unfit for consumption, to describe it falsely, even in terms of its nutritional value. The hygienic state of food shops is also regulated by this statute. In effect it codified the best practices of food and drug companies of the better sort, who were already in the habit of accurate and truthful labelling and the putting of their name and address on the back of the packet in case of complaints, not to mention including in the pack a slip carrying the packer's work number so that complaints could be traced to source.

It seems logical that legislation as it has grown has tended to follow existing 'best practice' and equally logical that the Office of Fair Trading, whose powers encompass the enforcement of the law on monopoly trading as well as consumer protection, should be advised by a committee which includes producers' and retailers' representatives, the Consumer Protection Advisory Committee with specific, if limited, powers under the Fair Trading Act. It is the responsibility of the Director General of the OFT to scrutinise trading practices to identify any which he or his advisors may decide are working to the disadvantage of the consumer. If and when they do, the Director General can ask the CPAC, which is an independent committee appointed by the Secretary of State for Prices and Consumer Protection, for a report. The report then goes to the Secretary of State and all such references are reported in the three government *Gazettes* in London, Edinburgh and Belfast. The contents of these references cover the trading practice and its effect upon consumers, relevant overseas comparisons in terms of practices and policies and any recommendation for legislation to remedy apparent unfairness. Thus a regular look at the *Gazette* will give people in business at least a glimpse of the activities of the OFT and CPAC.

This activity takes place under the provisions of the Fair Trading Act, 1973, which established the Office and empowered the Director General to administer and enforce the laws relating to monopolistic trading practices and consumer protection. The Consumer Credit Act, 1974, added to his powers and the functions of the Office now fall into four categories: consumer affairs, consumer credit (equivalent to the American Truth-In-Lending regulations), restrictive trade practices and monopolies and mergers. The Office also sets out to encourage trade associations and individual firms if they so wish to produce codes of practice in favour of the consumer. In Case Study 3 there is an example of a company which worked with the OFT in producing a code of good practice for footwear retailers. As the case demonstrates, they have profited by it.

The Office also has powers to proceed against persistent offenders such as mail order firms who either fail to deliver advertised goods or deliver substandard goods. The procedure followed is that the Office writes to the offending company requesting a written undertaking that the persistent breaches of criminal or civil law have ceased and will not be resumed. If the company or its management refuses to give such an undertaking, or, having given it, proceeds not to comply, the Office can obtain a court order forbidding the company to continue trading in the disapproved manner. A further breach will then bring an action for contempt of court, with a subsequent fine or even imprisonment if the judge feels that it is deserved. For businessmen and even for their managerial employees this is unprecedented. Whether the senior managements of most companies are fully aware of the powers of the OFT yet is impossible to say, but copies of the Office's own 'job description', *Work of the Office of Fair Trading*, can be obtained free and should be distributed to responsible managers.

The Consumer Credit Act of 1974 has been officially described as the most far-reaching reform of consumer credit law ever undertaken, in Britain at least. The United States Federal law was a few years in advance of it.

The roots of the new law on consumer credit lie far back in the development of case law on credit sales and hire purchase. Managers involved in hire purchase will not need to be reminded of the controversy about the morality of 'HP', permitting people to buy goods they could not afford to pay for in cash and perhaps leading them into debts which they could not discharge. In the bad old days there existed what was vulgarly known as the 'snatch back' or, more formally, repossession of goods on which payment had not been completed. When this happened, of course, the company selling the goods on hire purchase did not repay any part of the money which it had received from the customer, even if as much as ninety per cent had been paid. Between the wars there were many such injustices perpetrated in the name of business when unfortunate hire purchase customers fell ill or were laid off work and could not complete payment. It was this rather cruel enforcement of hire purchase agreements, as it seemed to the public at large, which aroused in 1936 a desire for the kind of protective legislation which came into force in 1974.

Under the Act the customer has a formidable array of new rights. Advertisements will soon have to carry full information about any credit offer, including the true rate of interest per annum. At one time it was not unknown for companies to state a rate of interest which was a flat percentage rate a year for a number of years during which the customer was paying off the principal sum. By the time the payments were nearing completion the customer was in reality paying an annual rate of interest at least double the original rate on the original principal sum. Also companies offering credit terms are now under a statutory obligation to give comparative information, showing all the alternatives which the customer may wish to study.

In the credit agreement which the customer has to sign the seller must give full information about the debtor's rights and obligations to him and the actual cost incurred by the credit sale. If the agreement is signed off the business premises, that is to say if it is a 'doorstep sale', the buyer will normally be allowed a 'cooling-off' period (a provision which existed under previous legislation in 1965) of three days during which he has the right to cancel the agreement without further obligation. The law says that the customer must receive a copy of the agreement immediately he or she has signed it. Originally these provisions were aimed at stopping the foot-in-the-door hard selling methods which intimidated or otherwise persuaded housewives to commit themselves and their spouses to the sort of agreement which gave the encyclopedia business such a bad name.

The other rights under the Act concern access to credit worthiness information held by the buyer about the customer, to have information about the state of his account, to pay off the hire purchase ahead of time and receive a statutory minimum rebate of charges and to have the agreement rewritten if a court decides that it is extortionate. Lastly, but important for the customer, is the provision that a credit grantor, a finance house for example, shall be equally liable for misrepresentation or breach of contract with the supplier of the goods.

The Act covers not only creditors, but equipment hirers, brokers, debt collecting agencies and credit reference agencies. All of them have to hold licences issued by the Director General of Fair Trading. The OFT issues a booklet called *Do You Need a Licence?* and any company involved in credit selling would be wise to consult it. It is unlikely that future governments will reverse the existing legislation, although it is possible, so this advice may remain relevant. As the Office says in its other leaflet *The Consumer Credit Act*, 'Unlicensed traders face severe penalties'. The OFT now keeps a register for public consultation of licensed traders, so your customers will be able to check whether you are registered. Copies are held in London, and in offices in Scotland, Wales and Ireland.

References

1. Yamey, B. S., *The Economics of Resale Price Maintenance*, Pitman, 1954
2. Pickering, J., *Resale Price Maintenance in Practice*, Allen and Unwin, 1966
3. Wilberforce, Lord, Campbell, A., and Elles, N., *Restrictive Trade Practices and Monopolies*, Sweet and Maxwell, 1966
4. McClelland, W. G., *Studies in Retailing*, Blackwell, 1963
5. Knox, F., *Consumers in the Economy*, Harrap, 1969
6. Galbraith, J. K., *American Capitalism: The Concept of Countervailing Power*, Penguin, 1963
7. Pei, M., *The Consumers' Manifesto*, Crown, 1960
8. Fridman, G. H. L., *Sale of Goods*, Sweet & Maxwell, 1966
9. Borrie, G., and Diamond, A. L., *The Consumer, Society and the Law*, Penguin, Third Edition, 1973

The July issue of *Which?* 1977 contained an up to date summary of the main statute and common law consumer safeguards.

Part II

The marketing response

4 Business policy and the consumer

The adjustment of business policy to consumer protection comes under the much broader heading of social responsibility. Of corporate social responsibility the economist and proponent of the freest possible private enterprise, Professor Milton Friedman,[1] has said it is 'fundamentally subversive' and could 'thoroughly undermine the very foundations of our free society ...'. For management to accept it as a policy would run counter to their duty 'to make as much for their stockholders as possible'.

However, it depends what you mean by 'social responsibility' in the managing of a company. The use of the phrase tends to cover everything from running a charities committee or setting up a scholarly foundation to treating effluent before discharge or landscaping a cement works. Like the phrase 'social marketing', which has come to carry the meaning of the purveying of non-profit services, there is a lot of room for interpretation in social responsibility. As far as consumers are concerned, the treatment of them as having long-run importance to the profitability and therefore the survival of the company is the critical factor. As Humble has remarked in writing of the *Social Responsibility Audit*,[2] 'Society increasingly and explicitly demands from business a more effective contribution to social responsibilities, even where this may damage short term profitability.'

In industrial societies business is the source of wealth and welfare, but in the past, and for that matter still in some cases, welfare has been and is made to give way to profit making. The public has now become very sensitive to environmental pollution and bad labour relations and is beginning to think about waste of resources. These are big social issues, and alongside them the protection of consumers can be made to look marginal if not trivial. In the micro-economics of the firm, however, the consumer is paramount, for without consumers there can be no market, and it is in competing for consumers that, in the long run, a good market standing for quality, reliability and service will count. An interesting consideration is that those companies which pursue progressive, pro-consumer sales policies are generally also those which have sound personnel relations and command respect in the business world for their profitability, growth and 'track record'.

In Humble's social audit the question posed is 'Has the company thought through "consumer policy"...?' Basically consumers are demanding four 'rights' from the company: safety of products, full and accurate information about products and services (without which some articles may not be usable and may produce sales resistance), a choice, and a voice. The purchasing power is in the hands of the better educated and therefore articulate and intelligent segments of the public, the professionals, like the founders of the Consumers' Union in America and of the Consumers' Association in the United Kingdom. It is therefore no longer sensible, if it ever was in the long run, to treat consumers in the old offhand way, to use sales tactics which leave them feeling that they have been 'conned' and possessing goods that they did not really want and which, if they cannot return them or receive compensation for them, they will warn their peers against, even if they cannot take legal action. A company with a record of consumer litigation is likely to find itself on the way out.

It is advisable, then, for any company making or selling consumer goods to develop and codify a company consumer policy. Kotler has pointed out that there is such a thing as the selling concept.[3] With this in mind the assumption is that maximum sales can only be obtained though an aggressive selling campaign, because left to themselves consumers will not buy enough of the company's products to be worth while. If the product is not satisfactory consumers will not buy it again, but there are many more potential customers out there waiting to be 'sold', and it is companies with this philosophy which practice the hard sell, which in its extreme form almost amounts to confidence trickery. As Kotler says, underlying this attitude to the customer is another assumption, that people soon forget their grievances, and on the whole do not talk about them for fear of ridicule or complain to consumer protection organisations.

It may have been the upsetting of that last assumption which incensed businessmen and marketers against the consumerists in the early days. The newer approach to the consumer is enshrined in the marketing concept. At the centre of this policy is the view that the task of the company is to seek out the needs, wants and values of a particular market segment and to set out to satisfy them more effectively and lastingly than its competitors, and as far as one can judge, this is the policy that works best in winning and holding markets.

The premises underlying the marketing concept are that the company mission in economic life is to define and satisfy a set of wants in a defined group of consumers. To this end marketing research must be used and the organisation structure must be such that the company responds readily to market changes and is sensitive to its target markets. In his celebrated essay 'Marketing Myopia', quoted in every marketing textbook, Levitt[4] highlighted the contrast between the two concepts. The selling concept concentrates on the needs of the seller to sell what he can make, to convert products into cash by fair means or foul, while the marketing concept begins with the idea of the customer's needs which the company sets out to fulfil with 'the whole cluster of things associated with creating, delivering and finally consuming it'.

Drucker[5] has gone even farther than Levitt with the notion that the very idea of marketing is to make selling superfluous, to provide products that are virtually tailored to customer needs in such a way that he wants to buy them without having to be cajoled or coerced. As he put it in *The Practice of Management*,[6] 'It is the customer who determines what a business is. For it is the customer, and he alone, who through being willing to pay for a good or for a service, converts economic resources into wealth, things into goods.' Thus the customers are the foundation of any business and keep it in being. Lose the customer and you begin to lose the business. It was Drucker,[5] too, who came up with the thought that the growth of the consumer movement was proof that American business had not been practising the marketing concept but merely paying it lip service. He added, 'Consumerism is the "shame of marketing" '.

Kotler[3] criticises the marketing concept for focussing solely on customer needs to the detriment of the environment and even of the customer's own health, analogous to the example that manufacturers of confectionery are giving sweet-eaters what they want but also providing much work for dentists. What Kotler calls the 'societal marketing concept', subsumes these additional factors and leads to the dictum that the company which adopts this policy actually rejects products which may not be in the best long run interests of the consumer, as has been the case with Marks and Spencer (see Case Study 5 in

Part III), and indeed promotes benefits of which the consumer himself has not considered. Again there is an assumption that consumers will come to their senses, and therefore to patronise, those companies which demonstrate the most concern for the general welfare of consumers. Oddly enough there seems to have been no research done into this possible outcome of business policy which might have provided evidence either way, although as a policy it could be the making or breaking of a company.

Kotler is one of the few marketing theorists to see that consumerism is 'the ultimate expression of the marketing concept' because it forces product managers and marketers to look at things from the consumer's point of view. By adopting this standpoint managers will be able to observe needs and values which have been ignored or overlooked by their competitors. In other words the pressure of consumer protection presents opportunities which, if seized upon by the company management, can provide additional strength for the marketing effort.

At the same time this change of strategy from the selling concept beloved of the 'hot-gospellers' of marketing, who relied on well-rehearsed sales talk to 'close' a sale, to the marketing concept is not just a change of philosophy and policy. If it is to work on behalf of the company in the modern environment, the thinking has got to permeate the organisation, and perhaps the organisation itself may have to change its structure to give more emphasis to marketing.

Because the marketing arm of the company is naturally in closest touch with the customers (unless it operates the selling concept and tells the customers what they want and what they are going to get, willy-nilly) there will be some resentment on the part of other departments which find themselves, as they would phrase it, 'taking orders' from marketing. But orders are what a company has to have, no matter who hands them on to whom. There tends to be a built-in conflict between the demands made on the company by marketing and the customary policies of, say, the production department, which prefers long runs, few design changes, large batch production, simple assembly and minimum quality control, to short runs necessitated by frequent design changes or small batch production for target markets, and very tight quality control.

It is probably this propensity to create conflicts of interest in departmentalised companies which has obstructed the adoption of the marketing concept in business, let alone strategic marketing with its additional burdens for senior management. When marketing first came to replace selling in the management vocabulary it was thought of by many managers as merely a semantic change, of American origin, and nothing more than a 'gimmick'. When a managing director of a British company had the functions of a marketing director explained to him he was amazed and indignant, what he heard sounded like his own job description, for the impact of true marketing upon business policy is profound and lasting.

The obvious solution to the organisational problem in bringing marketing to the forefront of the company structure as the sensing mechanism is the creation of marketing director or vice-president who can (under the chief executive who links the board of directors with senior management) negotiate on equal terms with the directors or vice-presidents responsible for the other key functions in the company. This move does not, however, obviate the fact that the marketing director will still be only one voice among many when policy decisions are being made, unless he has the backing of the chief executive and the boss understands the marketing concept.

In pursuing the customers' interests the marketing chief will inevitably want to introduce change, and change is unsettling and arouses resistance. When this happens, unless the company has worked out and accepted a considered consumer policy with which to guide top management, there is likely to be some waste of time and energy. A consumer policy should not be looked upon as a 'do good' exercise, nor even as a means of keeping the company out of trouble with the government, but as a programme for action which aids rapid decision making, gives flexibility to the product mix and product design, and smooths relations between departmental heads, or at least makes clear what marketing is trying to do.

An important handicap laid upon the marketing concept is that, when it is successful, kudos accrues to the marketing department, if the company is run that way. The resolution of this problem is to make the marketing concept the centre of corporate policy and to enlist the support of all functions in such a way that they take the credit for its success. A skilful, consumer-minded chief executive can easily ensure that this happens, but again only if he really believes in the policy. It will not work if he decides that the operation of the policy – that is the execution rather than the framing – can be safely delegated to his marketing director. Perhaps the organisation chart for a marketing-oriented company should be a circular one with marketing at the centre and the chief executive poised in a third dimension above it, having literally an over-all view.

Kotler[3] has the last word on this. 'The job of implementing a marketing orientation throughout the company is an uphill and never-ending battle. It calls for a commitment by the president, preplanning on how to sell the concept to others, and a continuous program of education and training.' More than that, when it comes to strategic marketing, that education and training needs to include a much larger proportion of consumerist information than ever gets into marketing courses at present.

References

1. Friedman, Milton, *Capitalism and Freedom*, University of Chicago Press, 1962.
2. Humble, J. W., *Social Responsibility Audit: A Management Tool for Survival*, Foundation for Business Responsibilities, 1973.
3. Kotler, Philip, *Marketing Management*, 3rd edn., Prentice-Hall, 1976.
4. Levitt, Theodore, 'Marketing Myopia', in Bursk and Chapman, Editors, *Modern Marketing Strategy*, Harvard University Press, 1964.
5. Drucker, Peter, *Management: Tasks, Responsibilities, Practices*, Harper & Row, 1973.
6. Drucker, Peter, *The Practice of Management*, Heinemann, 1955.

5 The concept of societal marketing

It is apparent from a thorough scrutiny of the marketing literature available to managers in Britain and the rest of Europe and the United States that for the most part the consumer is looked upon as a target, as a subject for 'consumer research' of a kind which is very different from the consumer research conducted by the laboratories of consumer protection organisations. In recent years, however, the consumer has been identified as an articulate, responsive, social being by some of the more broad-minded writers on marketing, but the traditional view has been that the influence of the consumer is felt by the firm through his or her purchasing power.

Writers like Brown, England and Matthews,[1] discussing the influence of the consumer, lay emphasis on the importance of who he or she is (no doubt classified in the market research manner by letter and number), what he or she buys and why, and when and where. Naturally this kind of information is central to the understanding of a firm's markets, which are made up of individual consumers. And such writers are at pains to warn their readers against taking a corporate egocentric view of the consumer or, worse still, the chief marketing executive and his advisers deciding for themselves what consumers want, as well as why, when and where.

The important differences between what has been called elsewhere the 'manufacturing' viewpoint and the consumer viewpoint is well brought out by Table 1. Straight away it can be seen that the production-oriented company is operating the selling concept discussed in the previous chapter. In place of seeking to identify and satisfy needs, the company tries to impose its preconceptions upon the consumer by means of persuasion techniques. In the past this has been quite successful, but with the extension of choice facing consumers, with more widespread education and higher education, and with the development of the consumer movement, it has become obsolete as a business policy.

Citing the report of the National Industrial Conference Board, *Why New Products Fail*, which was published in 1964 but does not appear to have been universally understood and taken to heart, Buell[2] makes the point that the majority of reasons for the failure of new products were neglect of marketing. In rank order the reasons given for failure by innovating companies were inadequate market analysis, defective products, higher costs than anticipated, bad timing of launch, competition, insufficient marketing effort, an inadequate sales force, and weaknesses in distribution. The NICB in their study also said that some company executives were frank enough to admit that the principal factors causing their failures with new products were mainly under their own control.

The marketing of new products is clearly a far riskier business than the marketing of established lines, but those established lines were new products once. It is instructive to reflect on the fact (not generally given much time or attention if realised at all) that established lines were new products once, and that they were successful, too. When companies succeed with new products and they settle down

Table 1 Model of the marketing concept

	Marketing-orientation	*Attitudes*	*Production-orientation*	
	Consumer forces dominate; emphasis on long-range planning	OBJECTIVES	Internal forces dominate; emphasis on efficiency and technology in the short run	
	Decision making starts with the consideration of the consumer	PLACE OF THE CONSUMER	Decisions are imposed on the consumer	
	Company makes what it can sell	PRODUCT MIX	Company sells what it can make	
CONSUMER	Used to determine customer needs and test how well product satisfies these needs	ROLE OF MKTG RESEARCH	Used to determine consumer reaction, if used at all	MANUFACTURING
	Create new markets as well as serve present markets	MARKETING STRATEGY	Satisfy existing markets	
	Focus on market opportunities	INNOVATION	Focus on technology	
	Sometimes lead, sometimes follow; offensive posture	COMPETITION	Always follow, react; defensive posture	
	An objective	PROFIT	A residual, what's left over after all costs are paid	
	Focus on marketing problems	OTHER CORPORATE FUNCTIONS	Focus on manufacturing and finance problems	

SOURCE: *Adoption of the Marketing Concept-Fact or Fiction?* by the Sales Executives Club of New York, Inc. (1967).

to enjoy the mature phase of the so-called life cycle, they almost certainly begin to forget their experience and disappointment with their failures. Yet failures are a rich source of marketing know-how for the company. Too much attention is paid to analysing successful product launches and too little to analysing failures.

The marketing-minded innovator puts the consumer first. He sets out to seek market opportunities and is pulled into the act of innovation by perceiving needs. The perception of a need which arises from a new technical development is likely to be biased away from the consumer and his actual needs (of which even he or she may not be fully aware) in favour of company investment in research and development or new product design. It is this commitment to an in-house development of a product which engenders a kind of marketing myopia not discussed by Levitt in his famous essay.

It seems, therefore, pointless to add to the existing mass of literature available to managers and entrepreneurs which extols the virtues and advantages of the marketing concept. By now there should be no one in manufacturing and retailing who does not understand the marketing concept. The fact that the organisation does not operate it may be due to a variety of reasons, historical, structural, or personal. And the result for the company and its employees will be a steady erosion of markets as competitors who have adopted the philosophy and put it to work attract away increasing numbers of customers.

The subtlety of this process of eroding markets through the alienation of customers is brought out by Thorelli, Becker and Engledow.[3] A transaction by a consumer, they point out, is not an instantaneous event with an absolute outcome; it is no more than part of a more complex and lengthy decision-making process. The act of buying something involves a series of decisions, depending upon the degree of understanding demanded of the buyer and the cost of the item which he is contemplating. Even when the transaction appears to be completed, the process of decision continues because the article bought will now be more closely inspected and perhaps tried out and, if found defective, rejected. Over a longer term there will be further decisions to buy or not to buy and they will have been affected one way or the other by the consumer's previous experience. Looked at like this, the act of purchasing anything becomes far more important to the producer than he might have made allowance for when he failed to put himself in the consumer's shoes.

Every potential customer will have to some degree a positive or negative bias towards making a purchase, influenced by previous satisfactions or dissatisfactions, and by those of family, friends and neighbours, as well as by advertising and other influences applied by the 'media' – those 'techniques of persuasion' so firmly denounced by Brown,[4] who appeared to believe that they had little or no power to affect long-term trends in tastes and preferences. Thorelli calls these preconceptions a 'stock' of cognitive content. We can perhaps see it best as the state of mind of an individual who has formed a set of opinions about our company, our products and those of our competitors. At this point – the point of decision as to buying or not buying a particular article – what the consumer needs is information. True, the decision can be hastened and the sale secured by some kind of pressure. But it seems that nowadays customers resent pressure. Perhaps they always did but were not mature enough to realise it or bold enough to evince it.

What may have misled some marketers in the past (the practitioners not the theoreticians) is the notion that only rejected goods are unsatisfactory. We cannot easily discover how many goods that have been bought and retained have proved to be unsatisfactory, but there are many reasons why a consumer may keep and use or use up something that falls well below his preconception of the satisfaction it was supposed to bring him. There is hardly any need to pursue these reasons, they are self-evident, but the fact remains that retained but unsatisfactory goods are a misleading factor in evaluating marketing achievement.

It was Dichter[5] who emphasised that a disappointed customer resents the feeling that someone has made a fool of him by selling him something that turned out to be a bad buy: 'We don't want to have the feeling ... that we did not shop or buy wisely'. This desire to be a successful purchaser is a matter of pride, and will probably be at its strongest among those consumers who consider that in making a purchase they have 'done their homework', whether that means asking around, reading all the literature or consulting a consumer advice centre. The corollary is, therefore, that the better educated and better informed consumers will take the greatest umbrage if they do not acquire the fullest satisfaction for their money.

Joyce[6] has listed the sort of needs which motivate consumers in their choices. Among them he includes a desire for social prestige, when a buyer may be attracted to a brand considered to be 'up market'; a need to be 'in the swim' or fashionable, perhaps meaning modern or youthful; the urge to follow a trend; the need to be thought a good wife or husband, or to be judged as a good bargain hunter and a judge of value. All these and other 'added values' he considers do contribute to the consumer's 'image' of the item he wants to buy, and Joyce, an advertising man, contends that advertising can build up such images and persuade the buyer towards particular products. This could well be true, in spite of what J. A. C. Brown has said, but it is the actual satisfactions that the buyer subsequently experiences which will determine his future perception of the company and its products. As Joyce concludes, 'Recall of the product, rather than the advertisement or slogan is what counts.' Indeed, for most people there is a strong desire for dependability, stability and consistency in their environment, and this desire should be taken seriously by those in business who are interested in winning and keeping customers. Furthermore we have to consider that there is such a thing as 'feedback' in consumer attitudes, whether in the form of a closed loop from his own memory of good and bad transactions (from his point of view), or in the form of an open loop from the recollections of others which have been communicated to him. And these feedback loops can extend over quite long periods, leaving the seller with an erroneous impression of success in providing satisfaction, while in reality the slow feedback will tell a different story.

Robertson,[7] in his book *The Lessons of Failure*, uses the term 'blind spot' for the inability of some manufacturers to see that they were running into long-term customer dissatisfaction by persistently poor quality of product but covering this failure up by means of selling techniques, such as premium offers, discounts, relaunches and all the surface paraphernalia of the selling concept. Such a policy may reap short-term rewards but the likelihood is that in the long run the consumer vote, in the form of cash flow, will be cast against the company which follows it. Some research into consumer expectations, attitudes and buying decisions or intentions has been done by Katona[8] and he has developed some techniques for predicting changes in direction of demand but not apparently a means of getting at the underlying reasons. To that extent the above comments must remain speculative, but there is evidence in the case material in this and other books that long-term customer dissatisfaction, of whatever kind, must have adverse repercussions on business.

The answer to this conundrum (which might not confront a monopoly unless adequate substitutes became available) lies in the application in business first of the marketing concept, and then, to reap the long-run advantages, of the societal (or social) marketing concept, which as we have seen goes deeper than the isolated satisfaction of consumers, and demands of the company and its shareholders and employees a greater measure of social responsibility.

References

1. Brown, M. P., England, W. B. and Matthews, J. B. Jr., *Problems in Marketing*, McGraw-Hill, 1961.
2. Buell, V. P., *Marketing Management in Action*, Pan Books, 1970.
3. Thorelli, H. B., Becker, H. and Engledow, J., *The Information Seekers*, Ballinger, 1975.
4. Brown, J. A. C., *Techniques of Persuasion*, Penguin, 1963.
5. Dichter, Ernest, *The Strategy of Desire*, Boardman, 1960.
6. Joyce, T., 'Advertising', in Ehrenberg and Pyatt (Editors), *Consumer Behaviour*, Penguin, 1971.
7. Robertson, Andrew, *The Lessons of Failure*, Macdonald, 1974.
8. Katona, G., 'Attitudes and expectations', in Ehrenberg and Pyatt (Editors), *Consumer Behaviour*, Penguin, 1971.

6 Marketing for tomorrow

The basic assumption of this book is simple (critics will be bound to say 'simplistic', taking the word 'simple' to be synonymous with simple-minded - in fact it appertains to herbs (simples) and not to simplicity!). It is that the prevalent mood of industrial society is sensitive to the activities of business, critical of those activities if not downright suspicious of them but equally responsive to the obviously ethical behaviour of exemplary companies. A rider to this thesis is that the ethical or responsible company will be successful in the long run, as many of them now are, and that those companies which do not follow this lead will not. For one thing, apart from the loss of goodwill and therefore of markets, their costs are likely to be higher *pro rata* as they belatedly try to conform to the demands of the consumer protection authorities and the criticisms of the increasingly influential voluntary associations.

Goyder,[1] in his book *The Responsible Company*, observed that (in 1960–1) 'the consumer needs greater protection and consideration than he can possibly get from the market', meaning the producers of consumer goods, and called for consumer representation on the boards of such companies. The nationalised industries, as they were constituted one by one (but not always so *ab initio* as with the Post Office) made provision for consumer representation. It does not seem to have worked as well as its proponents obviously expected. The various consumer consultative committees, as they are often described, are not so much consulted as consoled. When they have a grievance it is listened to and apparently considered by the board of the public corporation concerned, and too often that is all that happens. The decisions of the mammoth corporations are not much influenced by the consultative committees, and the reason for that deplorable state of affairs is that they are monopolies and behave as such. The government does not have the control over them that it was thought could be exercised when early exponents of nationalisation were making out their cases. Naturally enough the public at large were under the impression that 'public ownership' meant that they were to be the owners, and would have a say in the running of publicly 'owned' industries. In a sense they have, but the Nationalised Industry Consultative Councils (NICCs) as they are officially known have a comparatively small voice in the big decisions of the corporations. The Post Office Users' National Council for example, found itself supplemented by the much more vociferous private association, the Telephone Users' Council. The Information Division of the Department of Prices and Consumer Protection evidently believes that few citizens are even aware of the existence of the NICCs.

In their Consumer Information Bulletin, which goes to the press, they asked the rhetorical questions (N.21, January, 1976): 'What are the Nationalised Industry Consultative Councils? What can they do? Does the general public know enough about them?'. The posing of the questions suggests that the answer to the third one is no, and an inspection of the activities of the NICCs as reported in the Bulletin shows that while they can and do make successful representations to the corporations on such matters as safety (to which the gas boards are particularly sensitive), they have no effective say in pricing policy.

The National Gas Consumers Council, reporting in the spring of 1977, had to admit that 'We could not halt the two price rise proposals but we did win important concessions. We got a fairer deal for certain coin-meter customers and made some headway in eradicating certain regional gas differences.' They also managed to talk the British Gas Corporation out of charging for attending to gas leaks, but only for the first half-hour. Gas users had stopped reporting leaks for fear of heavy charges. This reactive instead of proactive behaviour seems not untypical of the NICCs, which only indirectly represent the consumer, their members being nominated as representatives of various voluntary associations and other such bodies throughout the country and appointed by the Secretary of State. This is not to say that they do not exercise some influence, they can and sometimes do obtain concessions, but that is all they are. The boards make their decisions which are communicated to the NICCs which then react. If they are to be truly watchdogs for the consumer, as they are often described, the procedure should surely be the reverse.

Goyder evidently had it in mind that some sort of consumer representation should be available in private enterprise, too. Some companies have long made use of consumer panels to discover patterns of buying behaviour and brand preference. This is not, of course, intended to be a form of representation, for the reports concern only existing brands and, according to Sudman,[2] are not always either full or accurate. The assiduousness with which panels keep their records and send in their responses also depends to some extent on whether they are paid (compensated, in the American style). True representation would mean that consumers would not merely offer comments on products, although that could be important and useful, but would also be consulted on new products and product changes. With the existing resistance to worker participation it seems unlikely that companies will want consumer representation as well. Decision making in business is already complex enough.

The practical alternative to direct representation, which begs a lot of questions about how it could be operated, is for the company to pay attention seriously and conscientiously to the published criticisms of its products or, in the case of retailers, to appoint consumers to an advisory committee, for which they would be paid. Such a committee then becomes an adjunct to the marketing function, providing a consumer's eye view which is not always available to the company in spite of the fact that they are all consumers in their private lives. There is a large retail company whose board of directors has said that the goods in their shops are good value because they buy and use them themselves. And that statement is partly true. They do use some of their own goods, and the others they try out on their staff, which is not such a bad idea. There is another company which has for many years manufactured a down-market product, which they could if they wished consume in the directors' dining room. They do not, nor is it offered to guests because, the directors have been heard to say, 'We know our market', and in marketing terms that is apparently C1 and C2 and, as everybody knows, company directors are A. It would be gratifying to add that this company is not very successful, but that is not so. There will always be companies which get by in spite of high-handedness towards the consumer, but it would appear that their number is likely to be diminishing.

A report from the Economist Intelligence Unit[3] has asserted that 'the private sector will, in the future, be operating in a much changed legal and social environment' and in the previous chapters we have seen the evidence of this in Britain and the United States and the European Community. Specifically on consumer affairs the report goes on to say:

> 'The movement to improve the consumer's position vis-à-vis the market continues to gather force. The

> consumer is now politically popular and the media have also adopted the consumerist theme as an important area of reader/viewer interest. Today no company marketing to the consumer can consider itself entirely free from scrutiny and possible challenge by consumerist activities or from the attendant glare of adverse publicity. Nor can it afford to ignore the potential effects of consumerism on its long-term future activities.'

The best move, therefore, must be to get ahead of the game and plan to stay ahead.

We have now seen in some detail how the rules of the game have changed in favour of the consumer, and sensed that any further changes are most likely to be in the same direction. Bartels[4] indicated this trend when writing about marketing philosophies in the United States in the early 1960s:

> 'Marketing is the conduct of that phase of business which is concerned with this determination and supplying of consumer needs, and therefore it is that management operation through which business fulfils its obligations to society in the role of consumers. Where this obligation is not recognized or where the responsibility to consumers is not fulfilled, marketing, in the fullest sense, does not exist.'

Since he wrote those perceptive words, the marketing scene has changed and is still changing. We have drawn the distinction between marketing and selling earlier, but it is as well to emphasise an additional, relevant distinction. At a time when salesmanship was the paramount consideration, consumers were seen as passive receivers of sales literature and sales talk, and of advertising and other similar communications directed towards selling. The seller held the initiative and saw it as his business to steer the consumer towards deciding to buy his goods rather than others, competitive or not. For a number of reasons, already arrayed in earlier chapters, this picture of the buyer-seller relationship in the consumer goods market will no longer serve as an accurate picture of what happens. The consumer is now also a decision maker of an active rather than a passive kind and much harder to manipulate. Indeed, any suspicion of manipulation tends to have an adverse effect and to provoke hostility.

The new type of consumer is sceptical and critical and has to be won over rather than bowled over. He or she expects consistent satisfaction from brands and will quickly desert the disappointing lines for others. As King has suggested,[5] using the consumer as a source of ideas for product design and content corrects any tendency to suffer from marketing myopia but at the same time introduces too many options without giving the manufacturer a clear directive. The classic case of this kind of 'over-marketing' was the Ford Edsel as described in Brooks.[6] The marketing research was painstaking and thorough, but perhaps the interpretation was not strict enough. In the event the new car developed into a design that tried to be all things to all drivers and in the end did not please many of them at all. The potential consumer must be treated as one factor in the product design decision, but never excluded altogether (oddly enough it has been done in the past, and will no doubt be done again). The way in which consumer needs and preferences are taken into account will obviously vary with the circumstances – improved product or new product, familiar market or new market, simple, low-cost product or complex high-cost product, domestic or overseas market, and so on. There can be no hard and fast formula, but the key thought is that the purpose of marketing is to build up the consumer's faith in the company and its products, whatever they are. In other words, to reverse to the company's commercial advantage the tendency observable in industrial societies in recent years to transfer trust from the producers to the consumer advisors and protectors. The company of the future will not be subject to the process, because the companies which are will not have a future.

References

1. Goyder, G., *The Responsible Company*, Blackwell, 1961.
2. Sudman, S., 'Consumer Panels', in Seibert and Wills (Editors), *Marketing Research*, Penguin, 1970.
3. Perrin, G., *The Changing Business Environment*, Economist Intelligence Unit, January 1975.
4. Bartels, R., *The Developing of Marketing Thought*, Irwin, 1962.
5. King, S., *Developing New Brands*, Pitman, 1973.
6. Brooks, J., *The Fate of the Edsel*, Gollancz, 1963.

7 The consumer as focus

That old saying 'the customer is always right' carried a ring of irony, for all that it really meant was that if the customer put up enough of a resistance when he was dissatisfied he would have to be allowed restitution in some form. The phrase is a carry-over from the days when customers were regarded as something of a necessary evil (and there are many in business today who harbour thoughts akin to this, and to talk to them of a new, militant and enlightened consumer will only confirm them in their attitude). The outcome of this attitude is that senior management concerns itself with the company, with production, finance and resources generally, and leaves the selling of its products to the sales department. This focus on the company as the centre of management effort has been mentioned earlier in comparison with the more modern marketing mode.

King,[1] having reviewed American management literature for areas of primary managerial concern down the years, decided that the production orientation began to be overtaken by what he termed the sales management orientation in the 1930s. No doubt the Great Depression of the 1930s was an important reason for this change. The author of *The Distribution Age*, Borsodi, writing in 1929,[2] remarked that the old formula for profitability, 'production; more production; still more production', no longer applied, and that the time had come for businessmen to take an interest in the channels of distribution. In the United States the emphasis in management writing began to shift from productive techniques such as work study to distributive techniques such as market research and advertising. The traditional superiority of the production department as the heart of the corporation began to be undermined. In Britain this shift of importance from production to sales did not take place till some time after the war, and even then, with sellers' markets persisting into the late 1950s, managements were slow to follow the American lead.

The more subtle move from selling to marketing was similarly slow and followed by a minority of firms. As has already been observed, the distinction between sales and marketing was thought by many to be artificial and merely another imported American technique which would eventually settle down to become part of the jargon of management. The idea that marketing is not just another word for selling (which takes place at the end of the process of design and production and is therefore inferior to both) was unacceptable or incomprehensible and as far from general business thinking as the idea that marketing should come at the beginning of the design and production process.

King goes on to quote a General Electric executive, Edward S. McKay, who helped to introduce the marketing concept into his company and who saw the marketing function as a series of consumer-centred activities, offering the chance to evaluate opportunities in the market by consumer research, to set objectives (this was well in advance of the fashionable MBO of the 1960s), to innovate successfully, to create a corporate strategy and to judge corporate performance. As McKay said, the traditional idea behind sales was that a product was planned and made and then given to the salesmen to sell. If they failed, management rarely blamed the product for being unsuitable, they blamed the sales department and its staff 'on the road' for insufficient effort. No wonder, as the idea that the consumer was central and not peripheral to company plans percolated through American business that there was talk and much writing of a marketing revolution.

Looked at this way, it is easier to understand and explain the slow and reluctant development of strategic marketing, which calls for an even higher degree of sensitivity and understanding of the mass consumer market. Indeed, between the sales management era and the marketing era (which is still developing in Britain and the rest of Europe) one might also identify a period when business, and its advisers, the consultancy firms were striving to gain a deeper understanding of the consumer by means of psychological techniques, to determine behaviour patterns, motivation and decision making. Business had realised the importance of the individual consumer and was trying to understand him, but had not yet moved fully towards the acceptance that to gain this understanding it was necessary to view the business and its products through the eyes of the consumer. It might almost be argued that the plethora of consumer research techniques acted as a screen between business and its markets in the shape of the consumers of its products. Certainly the first exponents of the new consumer research methods took little or no notice of consumerism as such. Their attitude to the consumer might even be described as mechanistic, which is inferred in the once current but now abhorrent word, manipulation.

The necessity of business to understand the consumer rests on the belief that the consumer is sovereign. Sovereignty is defined in the *Shorter Oxford English Dictionary* as 'the supreme controlling power in communities ... absolute and independent authority'. The economic concept of consumer sovereignty is that of a system in which there exists a free, fully competitive market in which the spending power of consumers determines the products and the characteristics of those products set before their eyes by obedient manufacturers. A moment's reflection reveals that this theory, which has been described as 'A fundamental precept of Western society ...'[3], is no more than that and has no substance in reality, because in the real world, (the one to which economists occasionally admit) the consumer does not have full information about the market, and such information as he does have is directed at him by interested parties who want him to buy something or to stop him buying something else.

Also in the real world there is monopoly, and not just the clear monopoly of a nationalised corporation or a dominant private company, but the monopolistic practice of branding and advertising to the point where the consumer believes that a product is *the* product, although if given all the information about all the available products he would realise that this is not true. It is information which raises the consumer's power to decide rationally what to buy and what not to buy. If this realisation jars on the feelings of businessmen and managers because they prefer that the consumer should know only about their wares and believe in them to the point of always buying them and no other, then they are not true believers in competition. But then, if business had always truly believed in the virtues of competition there would have been no need for anti-trust legislation and laws against restrictive practices. Therefore, in considering the consumer it is as well to clear the mind of such double-think.

It is understandable that the idea of consumer sovereignty should persist because it has been part of orthodox economic teaching for generations, ever since Adam Smith asserted in the *Wealth of Nations* that 'Consumption is the sole end and purpose of all production; and the interest of the producer ought to be attended to, only so far as it may be necessary for promoting that of the consumer.' But Smith went on to say '... in the mercantile system the interest of the consumer is almost constantly sacrificed to that of the producer, and it seems to consider production, and not consumption, as the ultimate end and object of all industry and commerce'.[4]

Mishan,[5] in his *Twenty-one Popular Economic Fallacies*, includes 'Consumer choice rules the Market'. He concludes that this fallacy rests upon the assumption that consumers have a full and informed choice, that it is this choice which in the end decides what is produced and at what price it is sold. He carries the argument further and includes in the true cost of a product the 'discommoding spillover' effects of, say, the motor car, on the environment. Satisfaction, he suggests, is unlikely to emerge from the profit-seeking activities of enterprise 'under existing laws', and recent legislative history tends to support this view. A clearer understanding of the real needs of the new, articulate consumer is necessary if more restrictions in the future are to be avoided.

Galbraith[6] has told us that the 'accepted sequence', the flow of instructions by means of purchases from individual consumer via the market to the producer, no longer holds true (did it ever ?). The mature corporation has the means to control prices, both of its raw materials and of its products. The producer reaches forward and controls the market and also the behaviour of the consumer, whom he purports to serve. This is what Galbraith calls the 'revised sequence', and marketing people will recognise that they do in reality try to operate that way.

If one studies a collection of marketing essays such as appears in Ehrenberg and Pyatt's *Consumer Behaviour*[3] it becomes apparent that marketers are in two minds about the consumer. On the one hand he or she begins as one of a group of enigmatic individuals whose buying behaviour responds to analysis and reveals patterns, so that they are no longer enigmatic but understandable. On the other hand consumers are seen as malleable and erratic decision-makers whose buying behaviour can be to some extent directed by advertising, publicity, pricing and the array of 'below-the-line' promotional techniques of persuasion. There seems to be little room left for sovereignty on the consumer's part.

In addition Knox[7] has pointed out that complete consumers' sovereignty would divert resources from capital investment into current consumption, and also that government intervention in the market by means of taxation imposes a third set of influences. Depending on our standpoint, therefore, we build up widely differing ideas of the 'consumer' but in fact none of us can be right because there is no such animal. Every consumer is different. One may generalise about consumers and be approximately right, for the time being, but all the time the nature of consumers in modern society is being modified. Indeed, as this book is designed to demonstrate, the consumer movement is just such an important modification not for all consumers but for a highly articulate opinion forming minority, which has grown up as a response to the attitudes outlined here. The root cause of the consumer movement is 'consumer dissonance', as it has been so nicely termed, meaning presumably dissatisfaction, disillusion, disappointment – the sentiments of all dethroned sovereigns. But the consumer protection apparatus which has been built up by the pioneers and their followers has gone a long way (in the advanced societies of the western world at least) towards giving consumers the strength in the economy which they were previously presumed to have and to exercise and which in some eyes, including even those of marketing men like Ralph Glasser,[8] is the natural counter-attack against the marketing apparatus.

Glasser, as a marketing man of long experience, is at

pains to expose the falsity of the view that the consumer is not the victim of a marketing conspiracy. Marketing shapes your life, he tells us and his view, expressed in 1967, is echoed by others from advertising, like Robin Wight[9] more recently (his book has the evocative title *The Day the Pigs Refused to be Driven to Market*) and Robert Millar,[10] a journalist, whose book suggests that consumers are affluent sheep rather than pigs. This kind of polemical literature, along with Baker's *The Permissible Lie*,[11] Turner's *The Shocking History of Advertising*,[12] Goulart's *The Assault on Childhood*,[13] and revealing studies like Pearson and Turner's *The Persuasion Industry*[14] and Tunstall's *The Advertising Man*[15] show how the tide of criticism has been rising against the supposed hidden persuaders (the title awarded the marketing men by Vance Packard[16]), the servants, or as Glasser would say 'high priests', of commerce.

We saw earlier (Chapter 2) how this backlash has tended to create a hostile environment for business, to the extent that it has put business on the defensive but not yet on its best behaviour as regards the consumer. Those allies of business, the teachers of management, have somehow missed this message, or have decided it was not worth relaying. Certainly there is little evidence that anything is being done to arouse the concern of business management for the consumer as the focal point of their economic activity. It is one thing to put the consumer in the spotlight, as the marketing researchers do on behalf of their clients; it is going to be a far better thing to illuminate the understanding of the consumer as an increasingly articulate and critical human being. The new generation of marketing men and women might like to build that into their marketing mix. It should pay dividends.

References

1. King, R. L., 'The Marketing Concept', in Schwartz, G. (Editor), *Science in Marketing*, John Wiley, 1965.
2. Borsodi, R., *The Distribution Age*, Appleton, 1929, cited by King.
3. Ehrenberg, A. S. C. and Pyatt, F. G., *Consumer Behaviour*, Penguin, 1971.
4. Smith, Adam, *The Wealth of Nations*, Vol. II, Macmillan, 1950.
5. Mishan, E. J., *Twenty-one Popular Economic Fallacies*, Allen Lane, 1969.
6. Galbraith, J. K., *The New Industrial State*, Hamish Hamilton, 1967.
7. Knox, F., *Consumers in the Economy*, Harrap, 1969.
8. Glasser, R., *The New High Priesthood*, Macmillan, 1967.
9. Wight, R., *The Day the Pigs Refused to be Driven to Market*, Hart-Davis MacGibbon, 1972.
10. Millar, R., *The Affluent Sheep: Profile of the British Consumer*, Longmans, 1963.
11. Baker, S. S., *The Permissible Lie; The Inside Truth about Advertising*, Peter Owen, 1968.
12. Turner, E. S., *The Shocking History of Advertising*, Michael Joseph, 1952. Revised edition, Penguin, 1965.
13. Goulart, R., *The Assault on Childhood*, Gollancz, 1970.
14. Pearson, J. and Turner, G., *The Persuasion Industry*, Eyre & Spottiswoode, 1965.
15. Tunstall, J., *The Advertising Man*, Chapman & Hall, 1964.
16. Packard, V., *The Hidden Persuaders*, Longman, 1957.

8 Consumer affairs as a business opportunity

In previous chapters we have seen some evidence that firms which have been considerate of the consumer in the past have reaped rewards and are continuing to do so. But company policy towards the consumer must be businesslike and not condescending, honest but not naive, and logical, basing itself on three now apparent facts, which were not always as obvious. These three facts or factors are, first that consumers are sceptical and always were when they could have access to the knowledge held by traders. Secondly, consumers have more knowledge than ever, and as a consequence have come to expect more of the goods and services they buy. It is impossible to write off nearly a century of developing consumer affairs with the suggestion that it is all temporary 'flare-up'. As we have also seen, the so-called flare-ups were repeated and each time were longer and more influential. The third consumer reality of the last quarter of this century is that consumerism is big and is here to stay, so we might as well study it and make the most of it as opportunity rather than threat. The threat attitude is merely negative.

In the United States the various agencies working on behalf of the consumer, including consumer advisers in business, have formed the Society of Consumer Affairs Professionals, a leading member of which is Mrs Esther Peterson, who was special assistant to the President of the United States (then Lyndon Johnson) in 1964, and then became Chairman of the Presidential Committee on Consumer Interests. She joined Giant Foods Inc. in 1970 as Vice-President of Consumer Programs and consumer advisor to the company president, a move which she herself has described as tantamount to joining the enemy, looked at through the eyes of the consumerist pioneers.[1] Mrs Peterson's friends did indeed accuse her of 'selling out', but the events which we describe in Chapter 2 and the improvements in Giant's marketing methods which took place subsequent to the recruitment of Mrs Peterson (who insisted as she says on having a 'hand on the levers of corporate power' as a condition of her appointment) – suggest that those friends were being as hidebound in their thinking as their opposite numbers on the business side who react against consumer protection.

It is the bringing together of the consumerists with business that is going to provide a formidable obstacle – many of the practices which consumerists would like to see universally adopted, such as unit pricing and open dating, do make costs higher and life a little harder for management, but not very much higher and not all that much harder. And the pay-offs in terms of consumer loyalty and increased business are there to be seen in the case histories in Part III. If consumerism is seen as a constructive force, then the natural hostility towards it begins to fade. There is one observation made by Mrs Peterson that should be more widely known. Her inside knowledge of the working of corporation policy and the forces lying behind the shaping of it led her to say, 'If I had had access to this kind of information when I was in the White House, needless conflict could have been avoided. Many issues could have been resolved in the market place rather than in legislative and regulatory chambers.' It is the recurring theme of this book that consumer protection as a separate, corrective force to business will go away only when business has made it its own.

The way Giant Foods did it with the help of Esther Peterson was to set up a Consumer Bill of Rights (the John F. Kennedy version), which we have noted earlier: safety, full information, a voice and a choice. A difficulty which many firms will face when they come to consider how best to implement such a policy is information of the technical kind which is supplied, for example, by Marks and Spencer's testing laboratories: the use of food additives, the characteristics of plastic packaging materials, the wearing qualities of man-made fibres and blends, and so on. With a wide range of products to handle such knowledge could be expensive to acquire (*could* be – although much of it is there for the reading), but it is possible, at little cost, to set up committees to advise on such matters from outside. Some companies already use academic advisers who are not professional consultants, but sometimes these are looked upon by the consumerist public (which includes other academics), as prejudiced by their role of advocate. This particularly applies to 'authorities' on food values, who will advocate, for example, artificial sweeteners at the expense of sugar, at the same time as one of their colleagues, perhaps in another country, is doing the opposite. The committee idea does away with this suspicion of bias, especially when the membership includes members of consumer organisations, government (or local-government) officers and, in the case of retail groups, suppliers. The marketing impact of publicising the existence of such sources of advice to the company can attract the attention of opinion formers and give the company an edge over its competitors.

The formula that works is simple, if a little hard to swallow. It is complete frankness in dealing with customers.

It is no use shoving the burden off on to a so-called customer relations officer whose unwritten job specification is to fob off complainers and to concede as little as possible. That is short-sighted. It is better business first to have standards of quality and reliability which will reduce complaints and after-sales service to a minimum, and to make those standards widely known. In these enlightened times advertising which highlights service to the consumer as central to company policy is going to pay off far better (again in the long run) that what has become the conventional persuasive message which carries only temporary conviction and, in some cases, may engender subsequent dissatisfaction.

Disagreement with what has just been said will be instantaneous among the marketers who have not studied the matter. It has been said that 'If the response to consumerism had been more intelligent in the past, consumer organisations would not be so committed to confrontation and legislation.'[2] There is no hard evidence that the benefits of a consumer-oriented marketing policy will always outweigh the costs, because no general research has been done to find any. There are two considerations here, however. There is the benefit and cost to the individual company, which is what matters in talking marketing. There can be little doubt that nationwide consumer-oriented company policy would be beneficial and reduce costs by rendering enforcement superfluous. But that will be a long time coming, and is a mere drop in the ocean of consumer spending, estimated by the Institute of Trading Standards Administration at no more than £25 million for 1977–8,[3] while total retail spending on consumer products of all kinds is given as about £35 *billion*, a proportion of about one fourteen hundredth in the pound. The significance of this calculation is that public consumer advisory and protection activities have room for expansion without making the burden on the tax and ratepayer significantly greater, whereas it lies well within the power of private enterprise to forestall any such expansion by adopting programmes of consumers' rights and thereby to secure a competitive advantage.

A useful concept to bear in mind is that of 'using the market as a source not a sink'.[4] This piece of advice was originally aimed at industrial innovators, but is equally appropriate to the marketing of consumer goods and services. Customers can be a valuable source of ideas for improving products and also for introducing new products. For example, if complaints are not merely rectified but classified and analysed as well there will emerge (not always but often enough to make the exercise worth while) a pattern that may have an important bearing on product design. As this kind of information is easily and cheaply obtained it is at least worth studying. It seems fair to say that hitherto the matter of communicating with the consumer has tended to be one-sided, with the producers concentrating upon advertising, public relations (of which press or media relations is a part), point-of-sale displays, brochures (for some services) and catalogues (for mail-order firms). The consumer panel appears to have been the only deliberate method of obtaining data on preferences direct from the consumer. The more random technique of market research surveys is less direct and relies on the testing of existing products using questionnaires which, however they are structured, are unlikely to draw out reactions of the kind sometimes described as 'deep' and which are sought in 'in-depth' interviews of a kind which are not normally practicable because of their cost. In any case, where it is the marketing arm of the company questioning and analysing the customers there remains the feeling on the part of the latter of being 'guinea pigs', and this is a very different sentiment from that of feeling in the counsels of the company, as members of an advisory committee should. This aspect of communicating with consumers appears to have been ignored in the marketing literature and in marketing practice by all but a minority of companies. But where it has been understood and has led to a more constructive policy of product improvement and product launch, results have been promising. More than that cannot be said at present. The 'state of the art' has not yet provided sufficient experience.

Straver has put forward the hypothesis that consumerist activity is a function of a number of social changes,[5] and he has defined eleven of these as economic for the most part (level of employment, wage/inflation ratio, product saturation – indicators of affluence in effect), but he includes the growth and availability of mass media and expands on this factor by suggesting that it is the amount of 'noise' in communication terms which now obliges selective consumers to seek clearer sources of product and service information. This gives the alert company the opportunity to employ advertising in a more rational manner, of the kind well described by a Cadbury-Schweppes group chairman, John Beasley, in the Advertising Association's *Advertising in Perspective*.[6] He sees advertising primarily as a medium of communication (admittedly *Sch... You Know Who* was a good slogan but it did not tell anyone very much about the product). He actually said in his contribution to the AA's symposium that '... advertising – again like all other factors – simply cannot be cost effective unless it is strictly related to consumer needs and wants', but, of course, those actual needs and wants have first to be identified. If a company were to gear its marketing to that strategy of seeking out and satisfying consumer needs and advertising the results of that policy, it is conceivable that that famous admission, still quoted and attributed to a chairman of Unilever, 'We know that half our advertising expenditure is wasted but we do not know which half', could be relegated to an anthology of outdated business clichés.

Beasley also says, and demonstrates it, that the key factor in marketing success is consumer satisfaction, again a recurrent theme in this book. When only four out of fifteen new products succeeded on a national scale (three were moderately successful but needed improvement), the rest failed 'because consumers tried them and found them wanting in some way'. The corollary is that advertising is far from being enough if the product or service fails to measure up to aroused expectations, and in those circumstances the advertising has been wasted, and it follows, too, that the company's investment in the designing, launching and making of the new products has also been wasted, leading to possible redundancy as potential markets shrink or are taken over by competitors. Beasley offers what he calls the cliché, 'The product must live up to the advertising claim and the advertising must do justice to the product'. The advertising industry used to have a slogan, 'Advertised goods are good', and there are still some newspapers who follow a policy of policing dubious advertisements. But the experience of consumers over the years has been that advertised goods were not necessarily good and could sometimes be worse than those not advertised. But the public, as we have said, has become more sceptical. In the *Harvard Business Review* survey,[7] mentioned earlier in this book (p.xxix), two thirds of *executives* surveyed thought that in general advertisements did not present a true picture of the product, or rather disagreed with the claim that they did. About forty per cent were firm that advertisements were not strictly truthful.

If the managers themselves are unconvinced about the accuracy of advertising where does the fault reside – with company policy or with the agency, or were the executives in question not all marketing men? Certainly the survey threw up the finding that misleading advertising was second among the dissatisfactions giving rise to consumer criticism (the first was rising prices, but not placed very far ahead of the marketing claim/product performance gap). Table 2, Exhibit II from the survey, highlights many of the grievances felt by American consumers and they will not be substantially different from those of consumers in other countries with advanced economies.

It is interesting to note that inadequate guarantees figure in the list, because these are the views of executives in industry and some of them will have not only drawn up the warranty documents but enforced them. Exclusion clauses have been a sore spot with consumerists for a long time, particularly in the motor car industry. A reputation for fair dealing could soon be punctured by the revelation that the manufacturer was, in effect, refusing to stand by the whole of his product's characteristics, because some parts of it had been made by another company. We have not found any instances of companies consulting consumers or consumer advisory organisations (such as the Office of Fair Trading's Department of Consumer Affairs) when drawing up guarantees. The underlying idea seems to be to play safe, like some insurance companies, and exclude as much from the warranty certificate (the policy, as it were) as possible. Here is another opportunity for companies to win customers – either by being liberal in their warranties or conditions of sale, or by not having them at all but making the brand name an all-round guarantee of quality.

The lesson of the *HBR* survey, now four years old (which may mean that the progressive thinking evinced by the executives examined will not yet have penetrated British business thinking to any depth) is that 'consumerism is good for consumers and good for business', and that companies can, by adopting consumer-oriented policies, use it as a competitive marketing tool. Eighty-nine per cent of the executives agreed with that, 70 per cent saw it as a chance for marketing to seize and only 10 per cent saw consumerism as a threat.

Table 2 Exhibit II Causes of consumerism's growth

Economic and social factors	*Importance rating**	*Business and marketing practices*	*Importance rating**
Consumer concern over rising prices	4·2	Defective products	4·5
Consumers feeling a growing gap between product and performance and marketing claims	4·1	Hazardous or unsafe products	4·3
Increased consumer expectations for product quality	3·8	Defective repair work or service	4·1
Deterioration in product quality	3·8	Misleading advertising	3·9
Political appeal of consumer protection	3·8	Poor complaint-handling procedures by retailers	3·9
Failure of normal marketplace operations to satisfy consumers	3·6	Advertising which claims too much	3·9
A feeling that business should assume greater social responsibilities	3·6	Deceptive packaging and labelling	3·8
Impersonal nature of the marketplace	3·5	Poor complaint-handling procedures by manufacturers	3·8
Greater concern over social problems generally	3·5	Failure to deliver merchandise which has been paid for	3·6
Consumers demanding more product information	3·5	Inadequate guarantees and warranties	3·5

*The importance rating is based on a 5-point scale, ranging from 'very important' (5) to 'very unimportant' (1).

Source: Greyser and Diamond, 'Business is Adapting to Consumerism' *Harvard Business Review*, Sept-Oct 1974, p. 44.

References

1. 'Consumer Affairs – Threat or Opportunity?', *Consumer Affairs*, J. Walter Thompson, No. 25, Jan–Feb 1977.
2. McRobert, R., 'The Cost of Consumerism', *Consumer Affairs*, J. Walter Thompson, No. 27, May–June 1977.
3. Johnson, D. W., 'Local Authorities and the Cost of Consumer Protection, *Consumer Affairs*, J. Walter Thompson, No. 27, May–June 1977.
4. Burns, T. and Stalker G. M., *The Management of Innovation*, Tavistock, 1961.
5. Straver, W., 'The International Consumerist Movement; Theory and Practical Implications for Marketing Strategy', Paper given at INSEAD, Fontainebleau, October 1976.
6. Beasley, J., 'Advertising in Perspective ... In Mass Consumer Industry', in *Advertising in Perspective in Industry and Society*, Advertising Association, undated.
7. Greyser, S. A. and Diamond, S. L., 'Business is Adapting to Consumerism', *Harvard Business Review*, Sept–Oct 1974.

9 Dealing with the consumer

We have considered consumer protection as a marketing opportunity and in Part III there is reasonable evidence that it can be a means of gaining a competitive advantage. It would be a pity to stand merely on the argument that this is the only reason for pursuing the consumer interest. There is such a thing as business ethics and reason to believe that ethical standards are rising and that companies indulging in unethical practices, even where they are not illegal, will come under increasing public pressure.

Brenner and Molander[1] conducted a survey of American executives on this very question, 'are the ethics of business changing?', and attempted a comparison with the findings of a fifteen year old study on the same lines. They did not find a clear-cut answer to their question, because their respondents were evenly divided as to whether ethical standards in business have changed significantly from what they were. They did find that managers in modern America are somewhat more cynical about the conduct of their peers than they used to be, and tend to favour the ideas of codes of practice, while admitting that codes by themselves will not accomplish a decisive change of behaviour. More important in the consideration of the consumer, although lower down their rank ordering of responses, is that the concept of social responsibility has become more acceptable and that the executives surveyed placed the customer ahead of the employee and the shareholder among those responsibilities. Respondents also affirmed that social responsibility in general will mean lower corporate profits in the short run but probably higher profits in the long run, but it was again a fairly even division with a narrow majority favouring long-run advantages.

Nevertheless the conclusions of these authors carry an important message for policy makers, or rather a series of messages beginning with the suggestion that the most direct way to restore confidence in business morality is fair dealing with consumers and employees. Corporate policy in this direction must of necessity come from the top and decisions should be tested against what is seen to be right rather than expedient, with the rider that self-enforcement of a code of good conduct is preferable to external enforcement, and that unethical conduct sooner or later becomes known outside the firm (the extreme examples we have seen in the past few years with the Lockheed revelations followed by the confessions of other multi-nationals. Peccadilloes may take longer to reveal themselves but are they worth the subsequent penalties?).

Ansoff, an acknowledged authority on corporate strategy, who does not touch upon ethics in his standard work[2] on the subject, does put forward the 'imperative' that in shaping a strategy for the future a company must 'monitor the environment for changes' and 'search for attractive product opportunities'. We have seen that the business environment has changed drastically in the past decade or so as regards consumer protection as well as corporate responsibility in general, and it seems as a corollary that the former is able to offer product and service opportunities to the wide awake and responsive company.

There is yet another way of putting this thought into perspective. Supposing your products are not consumer products but industrial, captial goods or equipment for sale to other companies in industry. In consumer goods, too, consider the selling of products to retail chains like Marks and Spencer which have their own laboratory testing facilities. It comes to the same thing. Here we are talking about selling to sophisticated buyers who do not make impulsive decisions and pay little regard to advertising or salesmanship. The important matter to them is 'does it work?' and 'will it work under our working conditions?'. If the eventual answers are in the negative the effect on future sales will also be negative though it may take time to show, which is the hidden danger of marketing sub-standard products to sophisticated customers. Not only will they be dissatisfied, they will also make known their dissatisfaction to others.

Consumers are not for the most part such analytical buyers of goods as companies, which after all employ purchasing officers with relevant experience. They are becoming more choosy, especially in the higher-income groups (although there is a gradual spread downwards here) and tend to take comparative testing and consumer research seriously, which is a strong reason for their turning to those retailers who also test and guarantee the goods they resell. The links between manufacturer and consumer have lengthened, as we noted earlier, making it more difficult for the manufacturer to have a clear view of consumer preferences, which is why he has had recourse to research agencies. They look at the consumer purely from the marketing viewpoint but there is no reason why they should not in future take into account the factors we have been paying attention to in this book. It was not, after all, a marketing research consultant who suggested Square Deal Surf to Unilever, but the then Board of Trade. Martin and Smith[3] have recorded that 'Unilever designed this to appeal to housewives who preferred more powder to a host of sales gimmicks and a heavily advertised brand name. The money saved from advertising was put into providing eighteen per cent more powder, although the price was kept at the same level as before. Yet, in spite of this clear value-for-money advantage, Square Deal Surf was not a brand leader. In fact, it came a long way down the list of Unilever's products in terms of sales.' This fact is not in the least surprising in the age of television. The unadvertised washing powder (there were a few introductory commercials in fact) remained on the market in spite of having to compete with the much more heavily promoted Unilever and Proctor and Gamble brands of detergent.

On this score it is interesting to note that the Monopolies Commission Report on household detergents[4] commented that the extra powder in Square Deal Surf packets was not looked upon by Unilever as promotional expense and the proportion of advertising appropriation saved was transferred to Omo. For those who think that better quality, greater quantity or better performance are in themselves sufficient to attract consumers it would be salutary to consider the exploded theory of the 'better mousetrap', so often quoted and attributed to poor Ralph Waldo Emerson, who is supposed to have asserted that the world will make a beaten path to the door of the woodland home of its maker. Not without knowing the way and not without knowing the object of the visit. As long as Square Deal Surf and its liquid partner Quix were not adequately publicised, the public would remain unaware of their advantages, and it was highly disingenuous of Unilever to pretend that it was some handicap on the part of the consumer that held down sales. No matter how good a product may be it will not survive the blast of competitive advertising in a highly competitive market, even if the counter-claims are specious and misleading – unless the powerful retail chains were to refuse to stock its competitors, which is unlikely, because they are in business to sell.

To that extent consumerism raises an important marketing dilemma, which is also a challenge. In Unilever's case supposing they had devoted all their marketing effort to Square Deal Surf, taking their stand on price and quality. Might they not have pushed Proctor and Gamble's rival products to the wall? Did the question ever receive full debate at top level, and if it did, what was the outcome? In *Consumer Affairs*[5] Geoffrey Batchelor of Lever Brothers writes at length on 'The Company Commitment' to the consumer, emphasising its Consumer Advisory Service and the emphasis placed on ensuring that all advertising and marketing claims for products are proved 'within the Company for technical, legal and general credibility', but makes no reference at all to the company's experience with Surf. All credit to the company for trying. The epitaph provided by Mr Batchelor is 'Interests will not always coincide – perhaps they never can', but Square Deal Surf lives on and that must prove something about dealing with the consumer.

This example may, perhaps, be evidence of the gap which still yawns between consumers and the most enlightened of conventional customer relations managers, and bring us back to a realisation that while there is a lot of marketing 'noise' in the communication system, rational deals based on clear information cannot fully succeed. At the same time it may help us to understand the reason for the very high mortality rate of so-called new consumer products, so-called because too often the newness is imaginary rather than real. Various estimates have put the rate of 'drop-out' of brands from supermarkets as high as 80 or 90 per cent over observed periods, but there is no way of knowing without careful research what lies behind such figures, how they are calculated or how signficant they are. King[6] says 'There is little doubt that most new brands or products do fail', and quotes an analysis by A. C. Nielsen over fourteen years which showed 54 per cent of new products withdrawn at the test marketing stage alone, with others withdrawn at later stages. An interesting addition to this depressing information is that these failures were not, for the most part, 'glorious bold attempts to introduce radical innovations' but 'very similar to those already on the market'.

A report by the American management consultants, Booz, Allen & Hamilton,[6] based on a 1964 study, gave a mean failure rate of 66 per cent for new products with little variation between sectors of consumer product manufacture, but when they had researched the fate of products launched on the market and of those shelved before reaching the launch phase the rate of success dwindled to an average of 1.7 per cent, with a slightly better score for 'consumer packaged goods' of 2 per cent. And the biggest advertisers who might be thought to have a strong advantage and therefore a better record showed a return on investment 0.9 per cent better than average in their industry.

Trivoli,[7] enlarging on this line of thought and contending that failure rates are a sign that consumer sovereignty survives, offers a supplementary figure – that in various sectors test market results show that one brand out of 23-26 succeeds. That is better, one supposes, than having those twenty-plus products fail after national launch. But is this really a sign that consumer sovereignty can be more than an abstract concept from economic theory? The theory assumes that consumers have rational and fairly precise wants of which they are conscious, and of which they make business conscious as a result of their buying power. As Knox says,[8] this is the basis of salesmanship, for consumers can be persuaded to change their buying habits, sometimes by the use of apparently objective descriptors and sometimes or simultaneously also using emotional or irrational suggestions. Here we face a paradox. We acknowledge that consumers know what they want and at the same time, unless it is our product they want, we set out to influence them in another direction. Now, as we have seen, consumers who have the knowledge to make up their own minds can do so, with the help of the consumer advisory agencies, who have no other axe to grind than that of protecting their members from exploitation – as they see it. To that limited extent the consumer is regaining lost ground, but he can never be sovereign in any real and practical sense. Consumer choice is limited by producers' decisions as to what to make. Ironically, the producers' decisions as regards new products and 'new' products (i.e. pseudo-innovations which are no more than window-dressing and style changes) are evidently largely wrong, but even that fact does not make the consumer sovereign, or capricious (as some disappointed marketers seem to feel at times), but merely dissatisfied and unconvinced.

Between the innovator, the manufacturer or the provider of a service, and the consumer there is usually a system of distribution: wholesalers, retailers, agents of some kind who do not always link the two chief parties to the transaction in a way which either can approve. The middlemen have their own interest, which is profit. Du Pont knew this problem when they invaded the footwear industry in the United States and later Europe with a new upper material which they called Corfam. It was designed to be a substitute for natural leather, since economic forecasts had suggested that a world shortage of hides for footwear would come into being towards the end of this century on such a scale that a more or less perfect surrogate would meet with a demand as vast as that for nylon. The story of the eighteen years and unknown hundreds of millions of dollars devoted to Corfam has been told in a number of places.[9] As long as the price of leather remained high, and technical problems with the 'poromeric' (as Du Pont named the new material (from 'porous' and 'polymer')) were not insuperable the shoe manufacturers could be sold on using it. Retailers, on the other hand, were interested mainly in selling shoes, no matter what they were made of, and were not prepared to spend much effort educating customers about the merits of a new material. This was not the main reason for Corfam's failure to capture a sufficiently large market to make it economical to produce, but it was a formidable barrier to acceptance. Another in this particular case, was that the consumers turned out to be far from homogeneous. The bulk market was for cheap, fashionable shoes for girls, and for these vinyl-coated fabric was adequate. Corfam could not compete with it on price. In some cases perhaps it is the retailer who makes the ruling decision on what is sold. Where a product does not give him a high enough return (such as the long-life sock[9]) he will not stock it. And if he disapproves of a product he will not promote it, if he carries it at all. To this extent the retailer is not always a strong link between producer and consumer and may even be a barrier. For all we know this communication channel, if it may be so described, may in part be a cause of so much new-product and product-improvement failure, and why some originators of products and services, such as publishers and tour operators, prefer to deal direct with the customer. Here is a key distinction between dealing with the ultimate consumer and dealing with industrial buyers. Advertising and promotional campaigns can convey part of the manufacturer's message to the consumer. The point of sale is where the acid test takes place, and we have seen how few products survive it.

As far as 'consumables' are concerned, providing that a product achieves a measure of acceptance and has a life cycle sufficiently buoyant to provide a pay-off within a reasonable period, there is no replacement problem. With 'durables' manufacturers have over the years come round to the policy of 'planned obsolescence', which for some time now has been a *casus belli* with consumer protection organisations (in the United States the controversy about the rights and wrongs of this method of keeping appliance sales moving is nearly twenty years old, a *Harvard Business Review* survey in 1959[10] revealed that many executives were uneasy about it). Vance Packard highlighted the matter in *The Waste Makers* back in 1960[11] but George Bernard Shaw had put his finger on it long before in his preface to *The Apple Cart*, when he invented the firm of Breakages Ltd whose role in life was to make sure that nothing lasted.

The other method, in addition to 'under-engineering' a durable product (a paradoxical description), is style changing or, as the cynics in the motor industry call it, 'badge engineering', making impressive but superficial alterations to the design, annually in the motor industry, less frequently in other sectors. Neither of these means of extending the life cycle of products has escaped the attention of the consumer advisors and it is more than likely that, with the growing emphasis on resource conservation, there may arise strong public pressures to discourage such wasteful practices by some means. Product differentiation, multiple pricing of a basic product superficially different but essentially the same, creating a set of false choices for consumers, appears to sail very close to the new legal winds and also, when exposed, carries with it the same opprobrium which attaches to all such chicanery and is potentially damaging to the company's market standing. Kotler[12] makes unambiguously clear what the intention of the selling company usually is in using this device: 'Product and service differences serve to *desensitize* the buyer to existing price differentials.' (Author's italics).

Economists tend to see product differentiation or variation (cf. Chamberlin[13]) as a way of segmenting a market with the aim of maximising revenue (the same basic product subtly varied to sell at a range of prices geared to market segments as identified by research) and at the same time raising the barriers to entry into a profitable market. It is more difficult for a competitor to attack a range of products at different price levels, advertised as different (sometimes not advertised but sold by mail order as well as retail) and made to appear different. If the competitor decides to use the same technique with which to mount his assault on that market, the result is highly bewildering for the consumer. The ensuing confusion and resentment create barriers to selling as well as competition (cf. Bain[14]). The consensus among economists such as Chamberlin, Bain and Knox appears to be that such marketing tactics, while highly profitable for the company using them, are economically wasteful and socially undesirable (although none of them says that in so many words, the inferences may be drawn). It seems to follow that a leading company publicly eschewing such manoeuvres in the increasingly critical atmosphere surrounding business today could reap an advantage commercially while also benefiting the consumer. This kind of issue is not widely discussed, at least not in the marketing literature. For marketers it would seem to be a legitimate means of increasing sales (varying product and publicity instead of price, especially where taxation is heavy – cigarettes and small cigars, drink, luxury goods subject to high VAT). For economists it has for a long time been an observable phenomenon to be analysed and understood as part of the framework of monopolistic competition – in plain words the attempt by enterprises to avoid the penalties of open competition. For consumers an *embarras de richesses* from which they can be rescued only by a flow of information which inevitably must expose the manoeuvre for what it is, manipulation. And the requisite information is now forthcoming, particularly for the consumers with the greatest purchasing power.

The more numerous and less prosperous will continue for a time in the state described by Caplovitz,[15] short of information (although it is there if not for the asking then for a small but worthwhile investment) and therefore a prey to the hidden persuaders as well as to the temptations of credit buying. Affluence apparently brings with it an increased desire to spend wisely (which seems paradoxical).

We may therefore assume that as the standard of living rises in an economy, so will the level of appreciation and of criticism. This rise will come about with the assistance of the media, particularly government-controlled television and radio, which have no interest in advertising (though in Britain not displaying any consistent policy as regards consumer protection), and the press, which has lost a great deal of consumer advertising to commercial broadcasting (the remaining lucrative areas are property, cars, fashion, cosmetics, travel and drink – and the editorial copy on these matters is somewhat suspect – 'commodity journalism' as the late Raymond Postgate liked to call it).

Ruskin, writing of 'modern manufacture and design' counselled:

> 'your business as manufacturers, is to form the market, as much as to supply it. If, in shortsighted and reckless eagerness for wealth, you catch at every humour of the populace as it shapes itself into momentary demand – if, in jealous rivalry ... you try to attract the attention by singularities, novelties, and gaudinesses – to make every design and advertisement and pilfer every idea of a successful neighbour's, that you may insidiously imitate it, or pompously eclipse – no good design will ever be possible to you, or perceived by you. You may, by accident, snatch the market; or, by energy, command it; you may obtain the confidence of the public, and cause the ruin of opponent houses; or you may, with equal justice of fortune, be ruined by them. But whatever happens to you, this, at least, is certain, that the whole of your life will have been spent in corrupting public taste and encouraging public extravagance. Every preference you have won by gaudiness must have been based on the purchaser's vanity; every demand you have created by novelty has fostered in the consumer a habit of discontent; and when you retire into inactive life, you may, as a subject of consolation in your declining years, reflect that precisely according to the extent of your past operations, your life has been successful in retarding the arts, tarnishing the virtues and confusing the manners of your country.' (*Sesame and Lilies*, 1871).

References

1. Brenner, N. S. and Molander, E. A., 'Is the Ethics of Business Changing?', *Harvard Business Review*, Jan–Feb, 1977.
2. Ansoff, I., *Corporate Strategy*, Penguin, 1968.
3. Martin, J. and Smith, J. W., *The Consumer Interest*, Pall Mall Press, 1968.
4. Monopolies Commission, *Household Detergents*, HMSO, 1966.
5. Batchelor, G., 'Lever Brothers: The Company Commitment', *Consumer Affairs*, J. Walter Thompson, No. 25, Jan–Feb, 1977.
6. Cited in King, S., *Developing New Brands*, Pitman, 1973.
7. Trivoli, G., 'Has the consumer really lost his sovereignty?', in Gaedeke and Ethcison, Editors, *Consumerism*, Canfield Press, 1972.
8. Knox, F., *Consumers and the Economy*, Harrap, 1969.
9. Robertson, A., *The Lessons of Failure*, Macdonald, 1974.
10. 'Planned Obsolescence', *Harvard Business Review*, Sept–Oct, 1959, cited in Packard, *The Waste Makers*, 1961.
11. Packard, V., *The Waste Makers*, Longmans Green, 1961.
12. Kotler, P., *Marketing Management*, Prentice-Hall, 1976.
13. Chamberlin, E. H., *The Theory of Monopolistic Competition*, Oxford University Press, 1949.
14. Bain, J. S., *New Barriers to Competition*, Harvard University Press, 1956.
15. Caplovitz, D., *The Poor Pay More*, Free Press, 1963.

Part III

The response to consumerism: Case studies

Introduction

In Chapter 2 we recorded a few examples of how enlightened companies in the United States have responded to consumerism in a constructive manner, 'taken it on board' as the cant phrase puts it, to their competitive advantage in spite of higher costs, but sometimes having to wait two years or more for the effect on their customers. It does not take much thought to realise that, with consumers as sceptical and suspicious as they are, a change in policy of an apparently open-handed kind will be greeted initially as just another marketing gimmick, and the message that it is not a gimmick but a genuine shift in policy, will take a while to sink in.

For more than six years now a large American advertising agency operating in Britain, J. Walter Thompson, has produced six times a year a bulletin called *Consumer Affairs*, mainly for client companies (there is another called *Consumer Affairs Bulletin* published by the International Co-operative Alliance, which has been established much longer and draws its material from the world press). *Consumer Affairs* keeps companies abreast of developments in the lively consumerist business, which is more complex and varied than is often realised. From time to time it publishes special issues, and the one entitled 'Consumer Affairs – Threat or Opportunity' has already been referred to in Chapter 8.

In that issue Mrs Esther Peterson recounted the new consumer policy of the supermarket chain Giant Foods Inc. of Washington, DC, and offered the following advice to businesses considering setting up a consumer programme: a 'cosmetic' programme will fool no one, the programme must have substance or it will fail; top management must commit itself to the principle of 'open dialogue' with consumers; the individual charged with designing and controlling the programme must work directly with the chief executive, and must have a voice in policy decisions; the programme should not be aimed at educating consumers but at changing the marketing policy for their benefit, and should have the power to change those things that can be changed (be they products or services), the right to explain honestly why some things cannot be changed, and access to the background knowledge to assess the difference.

The point of such a programme is to establish a dialogue which is a two-way exchange of ideas and not simply one party (the company) telling the other (the consumer) what a fine firm they are dealing with. Modern consumers do understand more than some businesses give them credit for and at the same time they wish to be understood by the business. It is those companies which set out to create a genuine two-way flow of information which are making the most of the consumerist opportunity, and not resorting to the defensive posture which results from seeing it as a threat.

The J. C. Penney Company, a very large retail chain in the United States, with some 700 outlets there and another 278 in Belguim of which 200 are franchises and 5 in Italy, has been in business nearly eighty years. The original Penney stores were run on what would now be described as consumerist lines, in that the founder of the firm made his own tests on the goods he bought for resale and later set up a Merchandise Testing Center as part of what he called The

Penney Idea, which was to serve the public 'as nearly as we can to its complete satisfaction' and to respond to the challenge 'Does what we do square with what is just and right?'. It sounds rather pious and paternalistic to a modern ear, but it was evidently good business. One may wonder, as a consequence, what made such a company set up a full-scale consumer affairs department in the 1970s. The answer seems to be that the group felt that it was time to systematise its approach to the consumer, and the outcome is that every Penney store runs management-consumer discussion of an informal nature and it is the department which sorts out for each store a representative cross-section of its customers for the manager to invite along. Each meeting is reported in detail to the consumer affairs department, providing an invaluable mass of comparative data on consumer reaction throughout the group, and at the same time increasing each store manager's sensitivity to consumers in his local community.

Describing this programme and commenting on it in the issue of *Consumer Affairs* referred to above, the Divisional Vice-President and Director of Consumer Affairs, Mrs Satenig St. Marie, observes that 'Most consumer research today is done from the marketing perspective' in an attempt to forecast consumer responses to the company's initiatives. At J. C. Penney such decisions can now be based on detailed actual knowledge of their customers, not as an aggregation of responses to marketing research but as typical local groups whose needs can be anticipated by analysing the feedback from their discussions. In addition the company supplies free consumer education material for use in local schools, and this material is non-commercial and objective, unlike much of the material supplied by companies looking at education as another branch of public relations, an attitude which has attracted adverse criticism from time to time. A recent study commissioned by the company revealed that 53 per cent of consumers are convinced that companies want to conceal information that might make their activities less attractive to customers, while 23 per cent thought that full information was withheld because companies believe that it would not interest most consumers.

As part of their consumer affairs programme, J. C. Penney took on to their staff a 'consumer advocate', a man who had worked in President Johnson's Office of Consumer Affairs and also at the Consumers' Union, and surprisingly he has the freedom to disagree publicly with them if, for some reason, it has not proved possible for them to accept his advice as consumer advocate. Thus he is able to maintain his credibility with the public at large. It is his responsibility also to bring to the surface consumer affairs issues as early as possible so that the management can give them full consideration in time to build into its policies an appropriate solution if that is what is called for. Such is the response of a large retail chain to consumerism in the United States. In their view businesses which persist in opposing the consumer movement are adding weight to the self-interest image which has built up in the public mind. Consumer affairs not only can be, but positively *is*, a sharp marketing tool – but it cannot be created overnight.

Mr T. J. Curry, the managing director of Currys Ltd, also writing in the same issue of *Consumer Affairs*, tells a similar story of a British company founded nearly a century ago. When his great grandfather founded the business there was no such word as consumerism in the language*, but the company was managed as if there were, the watchwords being 'fair trading practice', so that when the consumer movement began to make itself felt they were 'not afraid of the spotlight of consumerism'. Indeed they actually

* It does not appear in the *Shorter Oxford English Dictionary* of 1964, or in *A Handbook of Management* edited by Professor Thomas Kempner in 1976 (Penguin), but it is in French & Saward's *Dictionary of Management* in 1975 (Pan Reference Books).

welcomed it, priding themselves on having been leaders in good customer relations. Before the First World War when Currys made and sold bicycles, they knew how important they were to people in agricultural districts, but also that these people might not be able to pay the full price till after harvest time. Customers were therefore allowed interest-free credit for the period, provided that the agreement was honoured.

In the company's *Instructions to Managers* issued in October, 1916, appear the words 'Satisfied customers are the best business assets and no effort should be spared in obtaining as many as possible'. Admittedly those words have a familiar ring, and must have been used by many companies, but it appears that Currys meant every word and were not just mouthing a slogan. When they went into the radio business in the 1930s they established a Radio Research laboratory for testing and repairs as a back-up to their branch services and told their customers, 'Our interest in our customer does not end with the completion of a transaction; we are concerned with the continued efficiency of the article purchased, be it large or small'. Again they meant it, and were at great pains to see that no complaint went unattended. Of course, there were other companies, a minority unfortunately, which traded on similar terms, but not all of them would have responded as Currys did to the consumer movement, by setting up a central customer relations department with a brief to answer all letters, not with an acknowledgement but with a solution to the problem raised, within forty-eight hours. As Mr Curry remarks, 'We have always avoided commercial activity which gives short-term advantages', and 'it was our purpose to continue our reputation of being totally open with our customers'. To that end, in meeting customers' expectations they went considerably farther than was at any time demanded by law.

They really do have an astonishingly open-handed policy

in the Mastercare offer, which includes the Currys Price Promise. The latter means that if a customer finds after a purchase that he could have found the same article at a lower price elsewhere the company refunds the difference – but not if the cheaper item was a special offer of some kind. They merely want to demonstrate that normally a customer of Currys is never worse off shopping there than anywhere else. And, like J. C. Penney, Currys are interested in anticipating and preventing consumer problems. To this end the Central Consumer Relations Department monitors and analyses all letters and telephone calls from customers so that there exists readily available information about product and service areas in which complaints are arising. This does not mean that all their customer contacts are concerned with complaints. Two-thirds are requests for advice or help. Experience is beginning to show that such responsiveness on the part of a company, properly used as market intelligence, can lead to significant pay-offs in terms of goodwill and customer loyalty (it is a form of participation, and as such carries the same sort of impact as participation in other activities from entertainment to education).

Fornell[1] has made a study of American corporate Consumer Affairs Departments, which have increased in number rapidly in recent years, from less than ten per cent of a random sample of companies in 1955–8 to nearly forty-five per cent in 1971–4. Of the companies with an annual gross revenue of $1000 million about 40 per cent have established consumer affairs departments. According to consumer sectors the figures in 1974 for firms having such departments were 25 per cent in durable goods, 16 per cent in non-durables, 21 per cent in services and 18 per cent in retail.

These consumer affairs departments approach the consumer in a variety of ways. To assist in the improvement of buying decisions they disseminate information in the form of buyers' guides or informative labelling or instructions in the case of appliances (the latter may not sound new, but there have been some unhelpful instruction manuals in the past). Another way in which the departments influence the company is with the wording of warranties, mainly in order to reduce the risk to the consumer (it used to be common in Britain to word guarantees to exclude the customer's common law and statutory rights, but this will no longer be possible under existing legislation with effect from November 1978). The participation of the customer and therefore the closest and clearest communication link comes with consumer advisory boards on which selected representatives of the company's customers serve. The staff of these boards or committees – company employees with the consumer affairs department or whatever title is chosen – are also available to help the public. Some large companies even have a 'toll-free' telephone service so that urgent complaints may have consideration as quickly as possible (such a service is open to abuse, but experience shows that this is minimal – especially if the service is not publicised but made known only in special cases).

A limitation on the analysis of complaints as a monitor of consumer satisfaction is that not all consumers are complainers and instead of making the effort to complain they will switch brands (or stores), stop buying certain lines, spread their displeasure by word of mouth and for a time the company may not be aware of this happening. Fornell comments shrewdly that a small gap between expectation and disappointment may be bridged by the self-deception or tolerance of the customer, where a larger gap will not. Also, and there is an important warning signal here, an increasing sensitivity to quality is being brought about by all the various consumer advice services, including the progressive companies' services, which must lead to less self-deception and greater dissonance if firms permit or actually create these gaps between the promise and the fulfilment.

Buskirk and Rothe[2] have offered some guidelines for corporate policy. They begin with a separate consumer affairs department which has the power to monitor 'questionable practices', even when these are unintentional. The department's tasks will include the education of staff and managers and also the education of suppliers, or recommending the dropping of those which remain unresponsive. The department's costs are built into corporate overheads (what may be the savings in reducing or eliminating litigation is not easy to say, but individual companies should be able to assess them if they feel it worthwhile). The main result for the company is a much improved output of consumer information which may catch the attention of the opinion formers, indeed must given that the company believes in what it is doing and publicises its intentions and actions. The trade-off for business is positive action in place of government restraint.

The British scene reveals examples of responsiveness on the part of business to the consumer movement, and the following pages offer a selection of examples, not only of the response but also of firms which have anticipated consumerist pressures and therefore have avoided them and benefited thereby. The Consumers' Association have not made the assessment of company response one of their main activities, preferring to put their effort behind comparative testing and consumer advice of other kinds. They have analysed 780 cases of interaction with business in the years 1972-6, which include negative responses, requests for advice but also 45 instances of positive remedial action, involving design changes (15 to do with safety in tested appliances, two with safety in cars and four with safety in do-it-yourself tools, a total of 21). The remainder were changes in service arrangements, instructions and conditions of sale.

Of three major cases followed up in detail, two were Russian imports, the Moskvich motor car and the Russ cinematograph projector both of which were regarded as unsafe. In one case, the car, the makers asked their dealers to institute a pre-delivery check for which they paid. In the other the importers and the makers agreed to modify the projector according to CA's recommendations. The third case was a British electric mower made by a firm of powered lawnmower manufacturers who were trying to diversify. On receiving the *Which?* report they asked for a meeting with the association's expert advisers and, as a consequence, made modifications to all the machines which they had already distributed and to change the production design accordingly. They appreciated that their difficulties had risen mainly from their inexperience with electrical appliances. It is conceivable that the *Which?* report may have saved them not only from actions for compensation for injury but also from some adverse press publicity. Thus consumerism has begun to emerge as a part of marketing policy, a part which the company itself can undertake. If not, then the least the management can do is to take outside comments not merely seriously but positively.

References

1. Fornell, C., *Consumer Input for Marketing Decisions*, Praeger, 1976.
2. Buskirk, R. H. and Rothe, J. T., 'Guidelines for Corporate Policy', in Gaedeke and Etchison, (Editors), *Consumerism*, Canfield Press, 1972.

Case Study 1: The Travel Club Limited

'Good ethics is good business' says Irene Chandler, managing director of this small Essex company and, adds her husband Harry, founder and chairman of the company, it brings in business. The evidence of this is that customers of the Travel Club (which is not a club in the sense that only subscribers can use it but more in the sense that buying a copy of the *Good Food Guide* makes you a member of the Good Food Club) have not only been using its services for thirty years but their children and their grand-children, too, as they grow up.

In an industry remarkable in recent years for explosive growth followed by widespread bankruptcy accompanied, until the intervention of the Association of British Travel Agents, by the equally widespread disappointment and even desertion of customers stranded abroad, the Travel Club has an unblemished record of open and honest dealing.

Most, if not all tour operators, (no doubt following the custom of the carriers they use – the airlines and the shipping companies) make use of 'the small print', often elaborate booking conditions packed with exclusion clauses (some firms even state that they will not take responsibility for errors on the part of their own staff!). However, the

Chandlers have never set out any booking conditions. They give two reasons in explanation of this unusual if not unique policy. At first they were unaware that it was common practice to hedge the customer about with protective paper. Apparently they first realised that they were alone in not setting booking conditions when they read about themselves in the 'Consuming Interest' column of *The Spectator* as exemplary in this respect.

Secondly, once the idea had been broached, Harry Chandler's reaction was that he had prospered for twenty years on open dealing with his faithful clientele so why spoil things by behaving as if he had suddenly come not to trust them any more? The irony of his situation in an increasingly consumer-minded world was brought home by two of his customers, both professional men on good incomes who had had a good holiday with his company in Portugal, when they decided to complain to their local Office of Trading Standards about some of the wording in his brochure.

These complaints became the subject of an action against the Travel Club by the local office under the Trade Descriptions Act. Under this Act a 'false' and 'reckless' misdescription of a product or a service is a criminal offence. In this case among six complaints, three of which were dismissed by the judge early in the hearing, one concerned the phrase 'a few yards from the sea' which in fact was 120 yards (the distance of the villa from the beach) and another whether it was true that children could be seen playing on the beach from the windows.

It is interesting that Mr Chandler was asked by the Trading Standards officials if he would plead guilty, as it was quite usual. He refused on the grounds that he felt that the complaints were not justified and that in any case he had not made the claims recklessly. Indeed the court decided that 120 yards was a few yards in the circumstances described, and that the view of children on the beach not only depended on whether it was high or low water (it was the Atlantic coast, not the Mediterranean) but on the growth of the intervening hedge! The hedge had grown 18 inches between the writing of the brochure and the visit of the two complainants. Even so, the case cost the Travel Club £3000 in legal costs, not to mention the cost of a year's work by the Chandlers and a surveyor to provide the evidence accepted favourably by the Court.

The result has been that the company now 'undersells' its holidays abroad, to such an extent that customers come back saying how much better their trip had been than they had been led to expect, but some foreign hoteliers complain of the lack of 'colour' in the writing up of their amentities (for example, 'swimming-pool' in place of 'heated swimming-pool', because there is always going to be someone who avers that 60° Fahrenheit does not constitute 'heat').

It is worth setting out this incident at some length because it illustrates clearly the move towards *caveat venditor*, let the seller beware – even if he is quite honest. It must be emphasised, too, that this move would not have come about had vendors in the past been as honest as the Chandlers. Nevertheless they have prospered in an industry with a high casualty rate among the great and the small, with giants like Clarksons and Horizon collapsing along with literally scores of smaller firms, while the Travel Club pursues its policy of limited growth and good value for money.

The business details of the Chandlers' rise from a 1930s business with a few hundred pounds turnover a year to £4 million are given in Philip Clarke's *Small Businesses: How They Survive and Succeed* (David & Charles, 1972). In brief, Harry Chandler, a former shipping clerk on the East London docks, left his job to try running a one-man business taking people on holidays to southern Germany (he would take his bicycle and, while his older clients rested, scour the surrounding countryside for sights to see, then charter a taxi and act as guide). It was 1936, unemployment was high and war was impending, although few people believed that. The war, in fact, wrecked Harry Chandler's business and was the direct cause of its reinstatement.

On the outbreak of war, he was stranded with a small party in Switzerland (he had persisted in going when the other tour companies had cancelled). In his first profitable year he had also had to refund the majority of his customers in full (in an amicable settlement in a London pub they had let him hold on to their ten-shilling deposits to keep his little firm solvent!).

He spent the war in Army Intelligence in various capacities, among which was the repatriation of British prisoners from Changi jail in Singapore. They numbered between 2000 and 3000 and he kept their names and addresses. After voluntarily leaving a comfortable appointment with the Control Commission Germany (he and Irene, who worked as a cost clerk for Ford, Dagenham, made the tough decision together), he used the list for his first 'mailing shot', knowing that all the ex-POWs would have gratuities and might welcome a comfortable holiday in rural Switzerland. He used the Waldheim Hotel in Sarnen, where he had been stranded by the war for eight weeks and where the proprietor had lent him money to keep going. It is the first picture inside his brochure to this day, and there are literally generations of Chandler customers who go there. That is 'brand loyalty' of a kind that modern companies can hope for and could have, given the right policy.

Two other remarkable facts about the Travel Club which deserve to be recorded are that they gave up advertising in 1960, preferring their own direct mail campaigns, and they have never worked through travel agents, preferring their own direct contact with their customers. They are cautious, indeed wary, about growth. From experience Harry Chandler has calculated that true economies of scale in the travel trade cannot be achieved until a company has a steady 100 000 customers annually – and the gap, between their 25 000 and the economic figure, is dangerous territory into which they would rather not venture. Oddly, the company's telephone in Upminster now bears the STD number 25000, the number of their customers annually while back in 1950 when they had 5000 customers a year, their telephone number was 5000.

This considered policy of holding down numbers enables the small company (thirty employees, with a Board of two, recently increased to three with the promotion of the young general manager) to 'perfect the product', to give its customers the right holiday at the right price. They are 'up-market' in terms of price and product, again as a matter of policy, aiming at not being big but at being best in their market. Their policy of staying small extends even to the kind of hotels they use (they are also busy in the villa holiday sector), dealing mainly with hotels with 40 beds rather than 400. And they have resisted take-over bids from the jumbo groups like Trust House-Forte and the airline hotel companies.

If ever there was a customer centred service company it is the Travel Club Ltd of Upminster, but because of their recent experiences at the hands of the trading standards officers the principals, Irene and Harry Chandler, feel that consumer protection law is in danger of going too far. Not only because of the case brought against them, but they have also observed other tour operators proceeded against in different counties of England by different offices for the same offence and being fined £100 in one county and £500 in another. It worries them that legal opinion supports the view that an offending company could be prosecuted as many times as there are local trading standards offices. They do not deny the benefits which consumerism has brought and still believe that it is good business to put the consumer first, and are in a position to prove it.

Case Study 2: The Prestige Group Limited

In September 1971 *Which?*, the Consumers' Association's monthly report to members, carried a small item headed 'Bouquets'. It recorded that in response to a request for 'unexpectedly pleasant surprises' in dealing with retailers and manufacturers the journal had received 200 examples, mainly from readers whose complaints had been promptly and generously handled (few wrote to praise product quality, presumably because this is beginning to be taken for granted). Four companies were outstanding in their customer relations as represented in this sample – Marks & Spencer, Black & Decker and Witney each scored 2 per cent of the bouquets, but Prestige scored 4 per cent. Naturally the group marketing director circulated a congratulatory memorandum. Naturally? Some firms, fewer now perhaps than ten or fifteen years ago, would not have granted it such importance in their affairs. But Prestige are consumer-conscious, an attitude which stems possibly from their early experience of selling what some people regard as a rather daunting piece of kitchen equipment – the pressure cooker.

Their ten-year guarantees are simply stated, whether for their copper and stainless hollow-ware or their carpet sweepers: if during the period the goods show any defects arising from faulty materials or poor workmanship, and not from misuse or neglect on the part of the buyer, they will be replaced or repaired free of charge. Within the company, because of awareness that users sometimes damage equipment inadvertently through ignorance (although all appliances carry adequate care and use instructions), the policy is that if there is any doubt as to where the blame lies, the benefit of such doubt should go to the customer.

That a customer-orientated marketing policy is no handicap to profits and growth is well demonstrated by the Prestige Group's record. The Report and Accounts for 1976 shows a turnover of £48 million compared with £650 000 in 1946, two years before the Group went public. Even allowing for inflation that is an impressive growth record and pre-tax profits have shown a steady rise through the troubled seventies, the increase over 1975 being almost fourteen per cent. Over fifty per cent of turnover is earned in the United Kingdom, nearly £26 million in 1976, again an increase over the previous year of well over ten per cent.

The original company was incorporated in the United Kingdom in 1936 under the name of Platers & Stampers, and during the war years was engaged in munitions production. It did not get back to manufacturing for the civilian market until 1946. The parent company which established Platers & Stampers was American, Ekco Products, deriving its name from the initials of its Austrian founder, Edward Katzinger, a tinsmith by trade in his native country. He emigrated to the United States in 1881, worked as a mechanic for eight or nine years, then went to Chicago from New York and opened up a small business making baking pans for commercial bakeries. His business grew with the industry and the population, so that after ten years he was able to diversify into making equipment for confectioners and ice-cream manufacturers.

Edward Katzinger and his son Arthur, a technology

graduate of the Armour Institute (now the Illinois Institute of Technology), expanded the business constantly as their markets grew and as advances in manufacturing techniques were adopted. At first they expanded in Chicago, itself a growing city, then to Baltimore and New York state and in the 1930s to Britain. They were a highly innovative company and many of their kitchen 'gadgets' were protected by patent. In 1965, by an exchange of stock, Ekco Products was acquired by American Home Products of New York, one of America's hundred largest companies by turnover (about $800 million with the Ekco $125 million in 1965). AHP now owns about seventy-four per cent of the equity of the Prestige Group.

These three companies, AHP, Ekco and Prestige are not only diverse in their product ranges, which was a deliberate policy of their founders, but also concentrate to a large extent on kitchenware and domestic appliances generally. The Katzinger (the family name became Keating after Arthur and his father decided to adopt it) flair for innovation has evidently influenced Prestige, which brings in new products, like the recent Crock-Pot (a slow-cooking device which can be brought to the table), like most electrical appliances, the Crock-Pot at present carries a one-year guarantee. It is a simple enough electrical device but could easily be misused, whereas the majority of Prestige product lines are not so vulnerable (they did actually have one woman customer complain that one of their knives had cut her).

Prestige also provide retailers with detailed instructions on how to deal with faulty new products (replace immediately and return to wholesaler for stock replacement or credit) and faulty products which have been in use for some time (send to the Central Servicing Department at City Road, Derby, direct and not through the wholesaler, so that the customer gets early satisfaction). They will also deal directly with a consumer, and if the replacement or repair is free of charge (not the customer's misuse) the company pays the postal charges. Servicing charges are kept as low as is consistent with the costs of spares and repair time. The turn-round of repairs is aimed at being five days (working days), allowing for postal and other transit hold-ups.

It is part of company policy to regard product quality and product servicing as important to the long-term public relations or public 'image' of the company. The service department is a sensitive direct link with the customer. But servicing policy has to be shaped in the setting of company earnings, costs and profitability. The London office admits that it holds the view that a 'generous' servicing and replacement policy is beneficial (and the recent commercial history of the group seems to justify that view) but realises that among the numerous manufacturing units (there are nine in the UK alone, and seven overseas) there is likely to be a 'sterner' view, no doubt including the opinion that the customer is more to blame than is allowed for in head office policy.

In fact head office has come to recognise over the years that it is not unfair to the consumer, but less than fair to the factories who make the goods, to accept fair wear and tear in the guarantee period as a legitimate ground for free servicing or spares replacement. Today the company has excluded fair wear and tear from guarantee – for some users work a product harder and more intensively than others. There has been some misgiving in the minds of the group policy-makers that unqualified ten-year guarantees may be open to abuse but so far they have not shifted their ground.

Case Study 3: William Timpson Limited

Timpson are the second largest shoe distributing company in the United Kingdom, so that their recent reaction to the consumer protection agencies is of particular interest.

The Timpson Code of Practice, according to the managing director, Mr John Timpson, arose from two things – the first was his appointment at a time when he was conscious 'of the poor public image that existed within the shoe trade.' 'Whether it is true or not, the average consumer thinks that shoe shops sell shoddy footwear with unhelpful shop assistants who are particularly unhelpful when complaints are made.'

The second factor was the general code of practice outlined by the Office of Fair Trading: 'I realised', says Mr Timpson, 'that this was the vehicle that could form the basis of our drive to improve the whole of the service aspect of the Timpson business.' He was under no illusions about the difficulties of introducing such a code, because it entails 'the burden of putting the Company failings under the public spotlight', but nevertheless persevered on the grounds that his company was not entirely free from blame for the poor public opinion of the footwear industry, in common with the rest of the industry, and that he wanted to set and maintain higher standards in the range of shoes offered, in the handling of customer complaints and in the standard of service in the company's shops.

They switched the emphasis of their range from 'young fashion' towards more practical lines and in particular shoes for children, a highly problematic area for maker, retailer and parents, not to mention the young customers themselves. On the complaints side, they withdrew from sale all styles which had a history of a high rate of complaints, and introduced a new complaints procedure based on the promise 'If you have good reason to be dissatisfied with Timpson shoes we will give you your money back'. A grievance procedure supplemented this in the case of a customer whose complaint had been rejected by a manager, when the complaint was scrutinised by Mr Timpson himself, giving customers access to top management for the first time. These policy changes were incorporated in a television advertising campaign.

The code of practice, aimed at raising standards of service, was much more of a problem at a time when most shoe shops had gone over to self-service. To work out a suitable code and to make it easily intelligible to customers the company established a Consumer Relations Department, directly responsible to the managing director. A series of drafts of the code was produced and shown to staff, to consumer groups and to the Office of Fair Trading, who eventually endorsed the final document publicly.

The code covers legal obligations, complaints procedure, stock policy and customer information (both product information and after-sales care). To ensure that all staff were fully trained in applying the code there was a five-week course at all branches for part-time personnel as well as full-time. Display and point-of-sale material was designed to inform customers about the code. This included tickets and leaflets to accompany the product with the intention of ensuring that complaints did not proceed from abuse or lack of care of the product.

As the first annual review of the Timpson code of practice shows (published in November 1976), within one year complaints about their products had fallen by 25 per cent, while the national level of complaints remained unchanged (this is about 5000–6000 a quarter, according to the Office of Fair Trading). Also the percentage of sales represented by complaints fell from 4.8 in the half-year ending June 1975 to 3.6 in the half-year ending June 1976.

Timpson retail shoes from a number of different manufacturers at home and abroad. As might be expected the highest rate of complaints, as shown by an analysis they did in the third quarter of 1976, arises from ladies' shoes and from imported shoes. Because of their policy of withdrawing from sale shoes which have been found faulty by the company's quality control team or which have attracted an unacceptably high level of complaints, they have to keep their suppliers informed. In every case, their suppliers have agreed with the action taken.

Another innovation has been the introduction of a classification of footwear according to intended use; wet-weather, specialist (meaning sport and outdoor activity), heavy-duty, everyday outdoor, occasional outdoor (fashion) and indoor (party wear as well as slippers). If footwear does not conform to promised performance in its intended usage the customer receives a complete refund.

The company's policy now is to encourage the industry and the government, in the shape of the Office of Fair Trading, to sponsor a public education programme in foot-health, particularly for children. They also want to set up an extreme sizes register, even if it means directing customers to competitors who stock very large or very small sizes. Another objective is to standardise fitting gauges (even their own chain of shops uses three different kinds at present). They plan to work closely with local consumer advice centres and are introducing the 'Timpson Shoe Advisory Service' as a means of educating the public in the selection and care of shoes. This advice will be freely communicated to consumer groups, the media and customers. An allocation of £25 000 from the company's 1977 budget has been made to develop a method of testing Timpson footwear before sale, as a means to reducing even further the number of complaints. Technical skills for testing shoes before bulk purchase are, says the company, under-used, and they would like to set their industry an example (although they do not actually say that in so many words).

Timpson evidently see quality control, a high standard of service (including the proper fitting of shoes) and straight dealing with the customer as part and parcel of their marketing policy. They dubbed 1976 'Service Year', a slogan which appears on one of their staff training manuals. This particular manual lays down that Timpson shops will not treat any customer 'as just another person who has wandered into our shop', but that every customer shall be treated as a VIP, shown somewhere to sit, measured using a fitting stool and that every assistant shall carry and use a shoe-lift (better known to customers as a shoe-horn).

The practical marketing aspect appears in the instruction that staff must not 'let a customer leave the shop or lose a sale without asking for HELP from the Manager/ Supervisor/Senior Sales or any other nominated person'. The idea being that given first-class attention and service customers 'will almost certainly return to our shops'. It is important to emphasise the selling side of the code of practice to dispel the idea that Timpson are behaving as 'do-gooders' in the pejorative sense of that term. The object of the new policy is to build up business on a solid foundation of good customer relations based on good products, well selected and well served.

The retail shoe business is one of the most fiercely competitive sectors, and the 250 Timpson stores and 150 repair factories are contesting the many more outlets of the British Shoe Corporation. Part of their previous marketing strategy, in order to compete, was a 'self-service and fashion concept', and it was in this mode that management and staff were trained. As a company with 112 years of tradition (beginning with one shop in Oldham Street, Manchester) the previous strategy had been to sell sound (meaning durable) footwear to the C1 and C2 levels of the market. When the new managing director decided that it would be more advantageous to revert to this policy of quality and service there was naturally some resistance from the marketing managers and the sales force who at first thought it was a retrograde step. But now they see it was a positive move to forge a new, and true, identity against direct competition. With an annual turnover of £23 million at present and with sales growing and customer satisfaction clearly on the increase, there is every prospect that the new policy will pay off handsomely.

Case Study 4: United Biscuits Limited

The United Biscuits group of companies is a merger of eight companies, beginning originally shortly after the war with McVitie & Price and Macfarlane Lang and later including Crawfords, Macdonalds, Meredith & Drew, Carrs of Carlisle, Kemps and Kenyon Sons and Craven. There are numerous subsidiary companies in the group, including eight overseas, one of which – Keeblers – is the second only in the United States to Nabisco, the National Biscuit Company.

The oldest company in the group is William Crawford and Sons Ltd, founded in 1813 in Leith, and it is under that brand name that the group markets its Pennywise line of high-quality, low-priced biscuits. From its inception Crawfords always stood for good quality shortbread and biscuits made from the best ingredients and the Pennywise scheme would have pleased the founder. The biscuits are well made to high standards in the modern, automatic if not automated factories which have become integral in the baking industry. They are packed very simply in clear transparent packs, with no padding. The contents can be seen and counted by the shopper. These packs have been on the market since 1974 and sales are running at £20 million a year through grocery outlets, which the group likes to use. They claim an amazing sale of 1048 packets of Crawford biscuits 'per shopping minute'.

The company has never suffered a significant complaints problem with its products (they admit that biscuits are on the whole very simple products to make but the competition is fierce), but with the Pennywise line they receive virtually none because of the strong emphasis on good quality at a low price. The new line was launched back in 1974 and in 1977 one of the leading market research agencies described it as 'the most significant biscuit launch in recent years'. It has remained a market leader, but the marketing director, whose idea it was, insists that it was primarily a marketing move and should not be regarded as a piece of commercial altruism. As with other successful companies in the consumer goods industries, United Biscuits consider that if you give the customer a good deal you win and keep markets. The group now has 40 per cent of the United Kingdom market and is increasing this figure annually, on the basis that successful marketing hinges on value for money and reliable quality.

The British eat nearly six ounces of biscuits per head per week. In an inflationary situation food prices have risen faster than others, and are currently about twenty per cent. Taking 1972 as the base year (100), the 1977 Retail Price Index stood at 272 for grocery products in general, while for biscuits it was only 206. This holding of prices may be explained in terms of highly automatic production methods and very large production runs which have helped to counter the rise in raw materials costs.

The group chairman, Mr Hector Lang, takes a personal interest in quality control and admires the efforts of his friends the Sieffs of Marks & Spencer and the Sainsburys to maintain high standards in food retailing. United Biscuits are suppliers to both companies.

A high stock turn allows for fresh produce. UB aim at a

shelf life of one month for their products (they would obviously keep longer but UB's 750 salesmen making weekly or fortnightly calls on shops ensure that their products never have to live out their natural six months of maximum freshness). The group maintains a buffer trade stock of only two weeks compared with up to two months for other companies' products.

In recent years they have had to cope with decimal pricing, and now there is metrication coming UB packets already have the two weights marked although it will not be necessary till 1978. The group policy is not (and never has been) opposed to consumer protection. Indeed in introducing decimal prices and metric measures they consulted local consumer groups. At the same time they are beginning to find irksome some of the European Community criticisms about traditional names for biscuits. For example, that there is no cream in 'custard creams', which are filled with a flavoured mixture of fat and sugar. If the Brussels nomenclature is forced upon them, the group foresee an expenditure in changing packs and advertisements of around £1½ million at current prices. Their marketing men take consumer protection seriously enough and pay attention to the advertising code of practice (indeed they claim that they 'over-comply', scrutinising their television commercials in committee *after* they have passed the Independent Broadcasting Authority committee so that they comply with the 'spirit' as well as the 'letter' of the law) and to the Trade Descriptions Act, which insists that the word 'biscuits' appears on packs even when the contents are clearly visible and recognisable.

(Details of the group's history can be found in *A Fine Fell Baker: The Story of United Biscuits* by James S. Adam, Hutchinson Benham, 1974).

Case Study 5: Marks and Spencer

On the question of consumer reaction to their business policy, the executives of Marks and Spencer are apt to say that 'the consumer has proved to us that what is morally right is hardly ever commercially wrong'. In a book such as this, with a small collection of exemplary case studies out of what might prove to be scores if not hundreds in the United Kingdom, it was a problem whether to include M & S. Surely everybody knows about 'Marks and Sparks' and their open-handed treatment of customers with a grievance. A closer look at the company reveals what the customer on the other side of the counter perceives only as better treatment, good quality and competitive prices – and honest publicity.

Beneath this fourfold policy, however, lies a philosophy developed over the years. Simplified, it says that production and consumption are not separate economic functions but that manufacturer, retailer and customer are all parts of a single economic process in which each has a common interest.

Good quality is guaranteed implicitly by the brand name St Michael, and sustained by the work of the research laboratories (the first textile testing labs were opened in 1935, well before the development of consumerism as a 'movement' in Britain). The company takes quality control seriously and expects its suppliers to do the same. Given these safeguards the company then takes full responsibility for quality and performance, without resorting to elaborate guarantee procedures. Also the company has had a long-lasting influence not only on the production and testing methods of its suppliers but on their management styles, their treatment of staff (including training) and the conditions of work. The keys to the success of this liaison are long production runs, rapid stock turn and 'good housekeeping'. The company contends that the costs of substandard management are borne by the consumer.

This is an attitude of social responsiveness and responsibility that is a lot more than a fashionable tendency such as has been observed in many companies in recent years, engendered by a desire to foster a 'better image', to climb on the latest managerial bandwagon or in response to a senior executive's latest discovery in the United States. Marks and Spencer's policy of social responsibility extends beyond a fair deal for its customers to community questions such as the design and location of their stores, the economic use of packaging, the prevention of pollution and of waste of resources (they continue to be energy-conscious while most of the business world behaves as if the oil crisis were over) and the ensuring of safe systems of work without being harried by factory inspectors or medical officers. In short, the social audit at Marks remains a living issue and not a nice idea they had the other day but failed to implement. It was for this achievement that Management Centre Europe, the Brussels-based offshoot of the American Management Association, awarded M & S its first award for 'an outstanding contribution to the social responsibility of business in Europe' back in 1974. At the Copenhagen conference when the award was made the managing director of MCE remarked that the founding fathers of the business, Simon Marks and Israel Sieff, had paid 'fastidious attention' to the needs of their employees, over and above paying them a wage, before any self-interest had been realised. By 1916 when the original partnership was formed there were exemplary employers, mostly the famous Quaker confectionery firms like Cadburys and Rowntrees, but they were noteworthy by their very rarity. True, it became fashionable to label considerate employers 'paternal' as if somehow it were worse than the more usual callous indifference of the older, heavier industries. The fair treatment of customers is a concomitant of enlightened treatment of all participants in a business, but the majority of businessmen have never thought of customers that way.

Marks and Spencer approach the controversial business of advertising in the same spirit of enlightenment. While they have never based their business on advertising as some companies have done, they recognise that it has complementary uses to their policy of good quality, cleanliness and freshness (this applies particularly to the fast-expanding food business) but they spend about 0.1 per cent of turnover on such communication, including point-of-sale displays and the rest of the marketing paraphernalia, relying instead on the impact of new lines on an army of regular customers who soon show by their 'votes' whether they like the new product or not. An American woman shopper was reported by the *New York Times* as saying of one M & S store 'It's as if a bunch of Ralph Naders are running the place', the reason for which may be traced to the personnel department's slogan, 'The way you look after the staff is the way they look after the customer.'

The cynical view may be that Marks and Spencer with a £1000 million annual turnover can afford all this window-dressing but that smaller enterprises could never survive such generous, almost profligate, personnel and customer policies. The truth appears to be the opposite. It is the good relations built up over the years by such policies that has brought about the huge turnover from 252 stores and thirteen million weekly customers, who buy goods made by

500 supplying companies, 150 in the food business alone. Some of those suppliers have been providing M & S with the quality they demand for thirty or forty years, which suggests that the relationship between the companies is good, too, even though specifications are tight (so many stitches to the inch in a seam, for example) and the company's industrial management group acts as a watchdog over technological processes, engineering developments, quality and reliability, administrative systems (when M & S rationalised their own paper-work some years ago at a saving of millions a year, supplying companies were also encouraged to try it) and personnel management and welfare. Marks and Spencer employ a small army of staff managers, about one to every sixty employees out of a payroll of about 40 000. Each manageress knows her group by name so that interviews do not begin with a hunt in a card-index but with immediate recognition. Much lip service has been paid to such morale boosters, but in reality they are as rare as enlightened customer policies. Business on the whole cannot or will not spare the time and resources, mistakenly it would sêem. Another Marks and Spencer *bon mot* seems relevant here: 'If you give, you get'. To borrow from McGregor's celebrated study *The Human Side of Enterprise*, M & S practice what Theory Y preaches, as opposed to the repressive Theory X (crudely that people do not like work nor responsibility and must be driven and controlled). They are not the first to do so, but among the few.

(For a detailed history of the company see *St. Michael, A History of Marks and Spencer*, by Goronwy Rees, Pan Books, 1973).

Case Study 6: The Boots Company Limited

In Chapter 2 there is a passing reference to the marketing of drugs, both prescription or ethical, and the branded kind which used to be universally known as 'patent' because of the registration of their sometimes fanciful names. The purveying of nostrums, placebos, cure-alls and so-called household remedies seems to be as old as civilisation, or even older, having as it does some of the atmosphere of witchcraft and alchemy. It also seems that the human race was easily convinced of the effectiveness of an unguent, a draught or an elixir and that this propensity opened the door to a great deal of quackery and proprietary drug abuse. The author of *The Drugs You Take* (Hutchinson, 1966), Dr S. Bradshaw, a doctor with a long and varied experience of the pharmaceutical business, has described 'folk medicine' as 'a collection of myths, half-baked science, and other irrationalities', some of them as wild as Tom Sawyer's cure for warts.

He goes on to remind us that the peak of the patent medicines business came in the late nineteenth century, when 'advertising of them showed its wildest excesses' and the bulk of the sales was in the densely populated and unhealthy industrial cities. One reason for the great and growing market for remedies was the shortage of medical practitioners and the prohibitive cost to the poor of using their services. Another was that many of the people, indeed the vast majority, came from the countryside where they had grown up with the idea that aches and pains, boils and rashes, could be alleviated with the aid of herbs.

Jesse Boot, who founded the business of J. Boot in 1877 in Nottingham, came of parents who were country people and who, according to the centenary history, made a frugal living from making and selling herbal mixtures. Jesse began helping his mother in her shop at the age of thirteen, three years after his father died. It was he who added to the range of remedies some of the famous proprietary brands such as Beechams Pills and Braggs Charcoal Biscuits. He bought in quantity and sold well below other herbalists' and chemists' prices – for example, in 1884 he was able to offer soft soap at $4^1/_2$d for two pounds when his competitors were asking 4d a pound. Like his parents, but using ingredients other than herbs for some compounds, he made his own preparations, the forerunners of the Boots branded and BP products of today. Indeed the name he eventually took for his company, Boots Pure Drug Company, was a symbol of his desire to make exemplary products.

The influence of his wife, Florence, led to his extending the business beyond herbs and medicines and to the development of the now familiar department store side. But it is the way in which the pharmaceutical policy developed that is particularly interesting to anyone surveying consumer-minded business activities. There are many standard medicinal products and these are officially listed in the *British Pharmacopoeia* or the *British Formulary*. Those included in the *Pharmacopoeia* have a generic name, such as aspirin or paracetemol, followed by the letters BP. Over the years Boots tended to extinguish brand names, such as Regaspirin which was their soluble aspirin, and adopt the simpler generic BP names, in this case soluble aspirin BP. The same policy has been followed with household cleansers and garden chemicals. Kudos has become simply Boots Washing-up Liquid and Toxol Boots Greenfly Killer.

To ensure that retailers are aware of these developments the changes are listed in the company sales magazine. In March, 1977, for example, (Issue No. 423), there appeared an announcement that 'Over the years many popular Own Goods products have changed their titles and may have been discontinued. However, customers still ask for discontinued lines and refer to products by their old names', followed by a list of such products with their new generic names and another of withdrawn products, which included APC Tablets, Codeine Compound Tablets and others which have been found either questionable or for some reason undesirable. Many of the old-fashioned names for standard medicaments, such as Mylol (insect repellant) or Dermene (antiseptic cream) have now been abolished and replaced with the plain descriptive titles given here in brackets.

Customers do not all adjust speedily to these changes – for instance, although it was some years ago that Boots announced that their Wills Salts should be known henceforth as Boots Health Salts, they are still asked for under the established and familiar name. 'On the other hand,' a director wrote to me, 'sales of Family Antiseptic increased substantially when we gave up the name Supersan.'

It should be emphasised that this progressive and helpful policy has also been commerically successful. During the 1970s Boots have grown faster than at any time this century, with their aggregate shopping area increasing by over twenty-five per cent to at least four million square feet in 1977. This success cannot, of course, be attributed to the company's sensible and responsible policy about non-prescription drugs, but it seems fairly evident that it has done them no harm and the public, did they but know it, a power of good.

Case Study 7: J. Sainsbury Limited

Sainsbury's, as they are generally known to the public, celebrated their centenary in 1969, having grown from a simple dairy shop in Drury Lane, London, to an enormous retail chain with a total turnover of about £664 million and after-tax profits of nearly £13 million in 1976–7.

In the official history, *JS 100*, the period of expansion of the company which coincided with the centenary, and which was one of a series of such developments over the years, came 'as a result of its efforts to react with more sensitivity to the customers' needs'. This attitude has been traditional with the company since its foundation by J. J. Sainsbury, which was at a time when (as we have seen earlier in the book) food adulteration in the big cities of Britain was widespread. Sainsbury himself would have nothing to do with the tricks of the 'wicked grocer'. It was a time of general expansion in the retail food trade, with famous names like Lipton and Grieg as well as Sainsbury adding to their shops at such a rate that by the end of the century 15 chains or multiples had control of 45 per cent of outlets owned by the 80 companies in being.

Sainsbury pursued a policy of seeking out and stocking high quality provisions, which included Dutch margarine as well as the best Dutch butter (which after ninety years still comes from the original supplier, Buisman). However, with the development of the consumer movement they have also made a conscious policy of keeping ahead of legislation and of responding to public pressure for such things as open dating ('sell by' dates) and unit pricing as far as it is possible with goods that are not uniform. With such provisions they always give a price per standard weight as well as the labelled price.

This consumer sensitivity did not come about from a desire to jump on the consumer bandwagon nor from a calculation that it might pay off. David Sainsbury himself recalls that when his father and uncle decided to adopt a pro-consumer fair trading policy towards trading stamps they believed that for a few years they might actually lose money but they were determined to go ahead. In the outcome the policy had the opposite effect. They attracted more customers than ever and found, as other companies have, that public goodwill can produce tangible benefits in the form of profits.

As far as Sainsbury is concerned the customer is more often than not a woman. To keep in touch with them the company employs part-time counsellors, home economists or cookery writers, who lecture to groups, such as Women's Institutes, in particular regions, describing the company and its policies and receiving useful feedback from their audiences. The service began in 1970 and now there are nine JS Counsellors, one of whom, according to the *JS Journal*, the staff magazine, has given 500 talks in six years in the home counties.

It is part of the counsellors' responsibility to explain the company to the customer, including for example the extensive testing laboratories, one of the duties of which is to recommend the 'sell by' dates, which at Sainsburys are shorter than at any other firm in the food business. They even shorten the 'sell by' period on goods other than their own although they have a twenty-four hour delivery pattern and use refrigerated vehicles. The laboratories carry out about 60 000 routine analyses a year with a staff of 120 (of whom 50 are qualified scientists), some in research and development, others on quality control. It is a big investment, but valuable for the long run reputation of the company. 'We do not just stick a label on someone else's baked beans,' says David Sainsbury, adding that long run gains are bound to cut into medium term profitability, but are nonetheless worthwhile. Surprisingly they have found from experience that virtue is rewarded more quickly than the cynics would believe. Store hygiene, for example, has been a feature of Sainsbury's from the beginning. Someone once asked a Sainsbury why the company has got such a reputation for cleanliness and hygiene. The answer was simple: because the shops and stores not only claimed to be clean and hygienic but in actual fact were so.

Nevertheless they are realistic. Like other retailers they have been criticised for wasteful packaging, wasting resources, with such things as non-returnable bottles. The company did not ignore this reproach but studied the matter carefully and made a reasonable reply in a leaflet called *Sainsbury's Packaging*, in which, among other remarks they said 'in this competitive world no efficient manufacturer or retailer is going to incur more expenses that is necessary', so that over-elaborate packaging is unlikely, but a balance has to be struck between customer convenience and economy, bearing in mind that 'pre-packaging' (to use the conventional jargon) is designed to economise on labour costs within the store as well as to keep food clean and safe. It is worth quoting this leaflet here as another example of consumer sensitivity.

Wide checkout points for wheelchairs, calorie guides for dieting customers, recipe booklets, studies of car-borne shoppers (particularly women, who apparently dislike multi-storey carparks), point-of-sale explanations of ways in which to cook the cuts of meat on display, and numbers of other helpful ideas go to make up the Sainsbury way with customers. With well over two million square feet (approximately 213 000 square metres) in 1976 and a growth rate of $9^1/_2$ per cent in profits (when inflation is allowed for) over the past twenty-five years, Sainsbury have proved that being kind to your customers is money in the bank. Profitability has enabled them to invest £70 million from their own resources, in new developments in the past three years.

Index